# THE MONTANA MEDICINE SHOW'S GENUINE MONTANA HISTORY

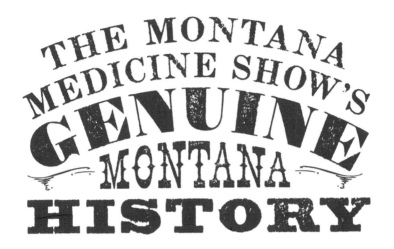

## BY B. DEREK STRAHN

RIVERBEND
PUBLISHING

## DEDICATION:

*For my supportive family—Katy, Ian, Alex, and Noah*

*Montana Medicine Show's Genuine Montana History*
Text copyright © 2014 by B. Derek Strahn
Design copyright © 2014 by Riverbend Publishing

Published by Riverbend Publishing, Helena, Montana

ISBN 13: 978-1-60639-075-7

Printed in the United States of America.

FN2019

Cover and text design by Sarah Cauble, www.sarahcauble.com

Riverbend Publishing
P.O. Box 5833
Helena, MT 59604
1-866-787-2363
www.riverbendpublishing.com

# CONTENTS

4

# INTRODUCTION

The historical vignettes that follow are a collection of radio broadcasts from *Montana Medicine Show*—a weekly program produced at the studios of KGLT 91.9 FM on the campus of Montana State University in Bozeman since 2008. Each two-minute episode spotlights a colorful person, place, or event associated with the Treasure State and its complex, remarkable past.

*Montana Medicine Show* is the brainchild of Jim Kehoe, KGLT's Music Director. Several years ago, he approached me with the idea of writing and recording brief radio pieces that feature snapshots from Montana history. Years before, KGLT—a listener-supported, alternative public radio station—had launched *Chrysti the Wordsmith*, a popular two-minute audio word study, which now reaches a national audience. Jim wondered if a Montana history program modeled on Chrysti's show might also have a broad, though somewhat more provincial, appeal. He likened the idea to an audio historical marker that, if successful, could transport listeners back in time through animated descriptions and engaging anecdotes.

The idea was intriguing, but honestly, I was skeptical. Though talking and teaching about history had long been a passion of mine, the idea of creating a fact-based narrative that could be read in under two minutes seemed daunting. I'd written about Montana history for newspapers and other publications before, but never for radio. I knew that simply telling an accurate two-minute story was challenging—researching and writing a concise weekly radio broadcast that someone might actually want to listen to seemed almost impossible. Besides, my voice sounded funny on radio.

To help bring me on board, and boost my chances of success, Jim solicited the editorial assistance of Barrett Golding, a successful radio producer, who helped get *Chrysti* off the ground, and more recently had been creating the weekly program *Hearing Voices* for National Public Radio. With Jim's vision, Barrett's keen ear for radio, and the technical know-how of KGLT engineer Brodie Cates, *Montana Medicine Show* was born. Since its inception, KGLT's general manager, Ellen King-Rodgers, has played an instrumental role is seeking grant funding from sources such as the Corporation for Public Broadcasting, the Greater Montana Foundation, Humanities Montana, the Gilhousen Family Foundation, and Friends of KGLT. The show would not be possible without the creativity, generosity, dedication, and good humor of these fine individuals and organizations.

Finally, I wish to thank my wife, Katy, and sons Ian, Alex, and Noah. Without their love and continued support, this project could never have materialized.

* * * *

Naming things is sometimes a challenge. A lot of folks ask me: why *Montana Medicine Show*? Engineer Brodie Cates came up with the name, and it just seemed to fit. Medicine shows were roving 19th- and early 20th-century caravans that traveled from town to town. They featured fast-talking showmen who peddled snake oil for a wide range of ailments, while also providing a wide range of entertainments—songs, dance acts, comedy routines, freak shows, and storytelling—to draw the crowds in. These part-vaudeville show, part-drugstore, part–circus-on-wheels were especially popular in the West. Lots of other name choice possibilities were less colorful, so we went with it.

The diverse, two-minute episodes featured on *Montana Medicine Show* are intended to be neither comprehensive nor groundbreaking. Though the program strives to inform and teach, its main objective is simply to entertain—to relate some interesting or quirky anecdote and, we hope, to give our listeners an enjoyable or thought-provoking glimpse of Montana's past.

Given the fleeting nature of radio, and the need to establish a quick impression, the episodes that follow are packed with colorful quotations and vivid first-hand accounts. These stories are necessarily compressed and, therefore, perhaps more sensational than lengthy and detailed accounts found in academic types of history. The reader may frequently be given the impression, as historian K. Ross Toole once observed, that Montana is—and always has been—"a state of extremes."

One is reminded in the pages that follow that while Montana's landscape is magnificent and extensive, it is also powerful and unforgiving. Floods, fires, earthquakes, and blizzards frequently take center stage here in the Big Sky Country. Likewise, its ever-unfolding drama is simultaneously shocking, poignant, gritty and moving. Like its vast mountains, its jaw-dropping booms and busts often defy expectations. As the uncompromising journalist Joseph Kinsey Howard said, "Montana has lived the life of America, on a reduced scale and at breakneck speed. Its history has been bewilderingly condensed, a kaleidoscopic newsreel, unplotted and unplanned…"

And at the center of it all—always at the center—are the people themselves. Montana's medicine show is filled with a raucous cast of hucksters, risk-takers, reformers, warriors, and reprobates. Here one will certainly find manly men and feisty women, tradition-clinging conservatives and reckless radicals. Yes, so-called "rugged individuals" have shaped this diverse place, but so have widespread grassroots movements and a pronounced governmental influence.

Some of these colorful personas, places, and events will be familiar to fans of western history. Some subjects have already appeared in the works of highly regarded Montana writers and historians like Dave Walter, Ellen Baumler, Don Spritzer, Kim Briggeman, and Jeffrey Smith, to whom I am greatly indebted.

But it is my hope that in these pages there might be a few surprises waiting as well.

KGLT radio can be streamed at www.kglt.net. To listen to episodes and get more information about *Montana Medicine Show*, go to www.montanamedicineshow.com.

*York stands at Louisville, Kentucky, levee in a monumental bronze sculpture by Forest Boone, in the Ohio River region he knew so well.*

# YORK

**York was explorer William Clark's slave and the first African American to cross North America above Mexico.**

Born in Virginia about 1770, York traveled with Lewis and Clark. He paddled boats, lugged provisions, stalked game—even gathered watercress for his master's dinner. Captain Clark reported: "my servant nearly exhausted with heat, thirst, and fatigue" and, later: "York very unwell from…strains carrying in meat and lifting logs…"

Clark sometimes ordered his slave to dance, which, he wrote: "amused the crowd very much."

Lewis and Clark displayed the dark-skinned and powerfully-built York to awestruck native peoples, who, Clark remarked, were "much astonished… and call him…big medicine."

### HISTORIAN JAMES HOLMBERG CONCLUDED:

*"His experiences undoubtedly altered his perspective on…his place in society."*

Once home, York requested his freedom. Clark refused. York became "insolent and sulky." Finally, Clark allowed York to join a slave woman he had married, in Kentucky, but warned "if any attempt is made by York to run off, or refuse to perform his duty as a slave, I wish him…hired out to some severe master until he thinks better of such conduct."

York remained a slave at least until 1816 and died of cholera before 1832. "York's Islands," near Townsend, bear his name.

*Jean Baptiste Charbonneau, "Pomp," rode much of the way to the Pacific Ocean in Sacajawea's Shoshone-style baby sling. This bronze sculpture by Jim Demetro stands in Fort Clatsop National Historical Park, Oregon.*

# POMP

**Only a baby, Jean Baptiste Charbonneau was a member of the Lewis and Clark Expedition.**

Born in 1805, Jean Baptiste was the son of Lewis and Clark's Shoshone guide Sacajawea and French-Canadian trader Toussaint Charbonneau.

Captain William Clark had great affection for the boy, whom he nicknamed "Pomp." Clark named "Pompey's Pillar"—near Billings—for the boy.

### HISTORIAN IRVING ANDERSON CALLED HIM:

*"America's infant explorer, whom destiny would later mark as an educated, cultural anomaly of the American West."*

Clark later adopted "the beautiful promising child." Pomp received "a classical education," in Saint Louis. He then traveled with Prince Paul Wilhelm of Wurttemberg studying plants and animals across Europe and North Africa.

At age twenty-four, Charbonneau returned to the America West. He worked as a trapper, interpreter, and guide for Jim Bridger and John C. Fremont. Overland traveler W. M. Boggs wrote that the young man "wore his hair long…[and] was very high strung…" but "it was said that Charbonneau was the best man…on the plains or in the Rocky Mountains."

Jean Baptiste Charbonneau helped blaze the Gila Trail, which became Route 66. He was a magistrate in Spanish California, and a gold miner in the rush of 1849. In 1866, at age sixty-one, he died while en route to the Montana gold fields.

The *New Encyclopedia of the American West* sums up his amazing life: "Charbonneau lived well in two worlds, while witnessing the unfolding drama of American expansion."

*Black Eagle Falls, which Lewis named when he spotted an eagle's nest there, looked like this before being dammed for electricity.* MONTANA HISTORICAL SOCIETY RESEARCH CENTER PHOTOGRAPH ARCHIVES, HELENA

# LEWIS AND CLARK'S GREAT FALLS PORTAGE

**Explorer Meriwether Lewis called it a: "truly magnificent and sublimely grand object which has from the commencement of time been concealed from the view of civilized man."**

The Great Falls of the Missouri River was also one of the Lewis and Clark Expedition's greatest obstacles.

On June 13, 1805, the Corps of Discovery first encountered these foamy torrents on the Big Muddy. The river plunged into a nine-mile-long chute formed by 200-foot-high stone walls, then cascaded over five separate falls—insurmountable barriers to navigation by boat.

So they had to go around. Moccasin-clad men harnessed to primitive wagons with tree trunk wheels heaved six canoes and tons of baggage over eighteen miles of brutal, cactus-strewn terrain. Lewis described the torment: "The men [have] to haul with all their strength, weight, and art[,]…catching the grass and…stones with their hands to give them more force in drawing the…loads…At every halt these poor fellow[s] tumble down and…are asleep in an instant…"

Stifling summer heat, apple-sized hailstones, menacing mosquitoes, rattle-snakes, and grizzlies made the interminable job even more hellish.

## TO LEWIS IT SEEMED THAT:

*"All the beasts of the neighborhood had made a league to destroy me…"*

It took the Corps eight trips—an entire month—to finish the ordeal. Finally, on July 15, the expedition moved upstream, toward an even bigger challenge: the Rocky Mountains.

*Lemhi Pass was where the waning theory of a Northwest Passage (by river to the Pacific) finally died, when Lewis saw this vista to the west.*

**Thomas Jefferson wanted to find a Northwest Passage—a convenient, navigable waterway to the Pacific Ocean—or lay the myth to rest.** His instructions to explorer Meriwether Lewis were clear: identify the water route best suited to "offer the most direct & practicable water communication across this continent, for the purposes of commerce."

In August 1805, the Corps of Discovery ascended Montana's Bitterroot Mountains. Near the crest of Lehmi Pass, they came upon what Lewis called: "the most distant fountain of the waters of the mighty Missouri."

### LEWIS EXALTED:

*"I had accomplished one of those great objects...which my mind has been unalterably fixed for many years."*

Lewis and his men momentarily rested, then became the first American citizens to cross the Continental Divide.

But his moment of glory was accompanied by great disappointment. Reaching the Bitterroots' ridgeline, Lewis saw no great river flowing to the Pacific—no easy portage to the Columbia—but rather "immense ranges of mountains still to the West of us with their tops partially covered with snow."

Jefferson's principal reason for the Lewis and Clark Expedition was, as historian Stephen Ambrose noted: "shattered by a single glance from a single man."

Journalist David Plotz was even more blunt: "[Lewis and Clark] failed at their primary mission. Jefferson had dispatched them to find a water route across the continent...but they discovered that water transport from coast to coast was impossible."

*Fort Union Trading Post National Historic Site, on the Montana–North Dakota border, has been carefully reconstructed. This is the Bourgeois' House, heart of the fort's trading business and administration.*

# FORT UNION

**Fort Union played a "starring role" in the Upper Missouri River Fur Trade.** For historian Merrill Burlingame, it was "the most famous fur fort of the northwest."

Built in 1830 near the confluence of the Missouri and Yellowstone rivers, Fort Union featured imposing watchtowers and towering 20-foot pickets hewn from massive cottonwoods in order to give "the impression of power, solidity and permanence."

### FUR TRADER EDWIN DENIG CONSIDERED IT:

*"The handsomest trading post on the Missouri river...."*

Saint Louis steamboats carried trinkets, liquor, and guns upstream to trade Indians for glossy beaver pelts and buffalo robes. One early observer noted: "They continually congregate here...sometimes coming the whole tribe together, in a mass." Historian Barton Barbour wrote: "the trade... made Indians' lives easier; but it also necessitated a reliance on exotic products from an alien, industrializing world."

Artist George Catlin, who visited the American Fur Company's "flagship post" in 1832, condemned Fort Union for introducing "contaminating vices and dissipations" to native peoples. "These traders," he wrote, "carry into these remote realms...whiskey and the small pox [and, in addition] are continually arming tribe after tribe with firearms...In this wholesale way...[the natives]...lose their better, proudest half...."

The Little Elk, a Lakota warrior, agreed: "We don't want to see any white people...because the goods the steamboats bring up make us sick...."

In 1860, 250 mounted Sioux attacked Fort Union, killing cattle and torching hay, lumber, mackinaw boats, and outbuildings before retreating. Tensions escalated. Profits plummeted. Finally, in 1867, traders permanently abandoned the outpost.

*Natawista Culbertson's Indian name was Medicine Snake Woman.*

*Alexander Culbertson*

# ALEXANDER CULBERTSON & MEDICINE SNAKE WOMAN

**Alexander Culbertson was "King of the Montana Fur Traders."**

Following his 1833 arrival at Fort Union, Culbertson advanced as a American Fur Company agent. He penetrated the Upper Missouri River Country and built the trading Fort McKenzie, near the mouth of the Marias.

Marrying Natawista (Medicine Snake Woman), the daughter of prominent Blackfeet chief Two Suns, Culbertson established diplomatic ties and a lucrative trade with the Blackfeet Nation. He and Natawista had five children.

Natawista assisted in negotiations with the Blackfeet, saying "I am afraid that [my people] and the whites will not understand each other; but…I may be able to explain things to them and soothe them if they should be irritated." Visitor John James Audubon described Natawista as "handsome…really courteous and refined."

Surveyor and treaty negotiator Isaac Stevens wrote: "[Alexander] knows every adult man of that tribe, and possesses unbounded influence over them."

## THE *PLEVNA HERALD* NOTED:

*"He was at the zenith of his power 35 years before there was any semblance of law and order…the only man in authority in these parts, and his word was law…."*

With Natawista's help, Culbertson negotiated treaties and blazed transportation networks, and founded Fort Benton—Montana's first permanent settlement.

*The side-wheeler* Yellow Stone, *launched in 1831, was similar to the* St. Peters, *which delivered smallpox-infected goods to Fort Union (also shown here) in 1837. Art by Robert Black.*

*Many Plains Indian tribes recorded 1837 as the year of smallpox with the disease's characteristic spots that left deep scars. Clockwise from above left, illustrations for 1837 from a Blackfoot winter count on a bison robe, from Bull Plume's (Blackfoot) winter count, and from a Lakota (Sioux) winter count.*

# 1837 SMALLPOX EPIDEMIC

**The S.S. *St. Peters*, an American Fur Company steamboat, carried trade goods to the native peoples on the Upper Missouri River. In 1837 it also carried an unintended cargo: smallpox and death for thousands of Northern Plains Indians.**

Company personnel tried to inoculate Indians living near Fort Union, but it was in vain. When tribes fled, the smallpox spread with them westward and into Canada. Fur company bookkeeper Edwin Denig later wrote: "They scattered through the mountains in the hope of running away from the pestilence. All order was lost. No one pretended to lead or advise. The sick and the dead were left for the wolves and each family tried to save itself."

Fur trader Charles Larpenteur said it was "awful—the scene…where some went crazy, and others were half eaten up by maggots before they died."

At the Missouri's headwaters, trader Alexander Culbertson arrived at a major Blackfeet encampment and found only two survivors. Horrified, he described how "[h]undreds of decaying forms of human beings, horses, and dogs, lay scattered everywhere among the lodges."

The epidemic continued until winter, killing an estimated two thirds of the Blackfeet, one half of the Assiniboines and Arikaras, a third of the Crows, and a quarter of the Pawnees.

### HISTORIAN HIRAM CHITTENDEN DESCRIBED THE EPIDEMIC AS:

*"mortality almost without parallel in the history of plagues."*

*Sacrifice Cliff rises above the Yellowstone River near Billings.*

# SACRIFICE CLIFF

**A 200-foot landmark dominates the skyline southeast of present Billings: the Sacrifice Cliff.**

The Crow people call it "The-place-of-skulls" or "The-place-where-the-white-horse-went-down."

In the later 1830s, smallpox decimated Montana's Indians in one of North America's most catastrophic epidemics. Anthropologist W. Raymond Wood wrote: "There is nothing in our experience we can compare it to… It was completely devastating."

Two young Crow warriors returned from a horse-stealing expedition to find "their friends, relatives and countrymen all motionless in death."

Trapper Thomas LaForge said, "Friends were abandoning the fallen ones and fleeing in all directions…These two men discussed…their forlorn situation…[and] agreed upon a double suicide."

Crow storyteller Old Coyote recalled: "They took out their best clothes and put them on…they went up to the cliff and rode [double on a snow white horse] along the rimrocks singing their [death] songs. Then they blindfolded the horse and turned toward the edge of the cliff…They were still singing when the horse went over…" A group of teenagers witnessed the suicide.

### CROW CHIEF PLENTY COUPS
### LATER DECLARED:

*"That spot is big medicine…My uncle told me the smallpox ceased its torment on the day the two young men rode over the bluff."*

*Although there is no known picture of Running Eagle, George Catlin painted this Blackfeet woman in 1832; the warrior woman, her contemporary, may have worn similar traditional clothing.*

# RUNNING EAGLE

**Brown Weasel Woman—later known as Running Eagle—was "the Joan of Arc of the Blackfeet people."**

Born about 1820, she soon expressed a dislike for traditional female duties. Her father—a noted warrior—raised her as a Ninawaki or "manly hearted woman." Professor Lisa Aldred says they "were characterized by assertiveness, independence, property ownership, and leadership."

The ideal Blackfeet woman then was quiet, submissive, and private. But Brown Weasel Woman preferred killing buffalo and singlehandedly stealing horses. In an act of great bravery, she saved her father from certain death when enemies shot his horse.

### HISTORIAN HUGH DEMPSEY WROTE:

*After she...killed an enemy in battle she was given the man's name Running Eagle. She was said to have been the only woman in the history of the tribe so honored.*

Running Eagle joined a warrior society and became a war chief. On the warpath, ignoring the objections of her male followers, she also cooked and repaired moccasins, stating flatly: "I am a woman. Men don't know how to sew."

In the 1840s, fur trader John Rowand likely encountered Running Eagle in Cree country. He described: "a war party of 1,000 men who had...at their head the Queen of the Plains."

Salish warriors killed Running Eagle during a horse-stealing raid in about 1850. Author James Willard Schultz later immortalized her life in his dramatic novel, *Running Eagle: The Warrior Girl*.

A waterfall in Glacier National Park bears her name.

*Energetic Father Pierre DeSmet seems ready to leap to action in this photo-graphic portrait.*

# FATHER DeSMET

**Father Pierre Jean DeSmet was known as "the Apostle of the Rocky Mountains," but to native peoples he was simply "Black Robe."**

DeSmet was born in 1801 in Belgium. In 1840, he began what the Oxford History of the American West deemed: "the grandest missionary work of the nineteenth century…"

DeSmet followed Lewis and Clark's route up the Missouri River. In the Bitterroot Valley, near present-day Stevensville, he established St. Mary's Mission—Montana's first permanent non-native settlement.

DeSmet recalled: "[The Indians] came from all parts and from great distances to meet me…and present all their young children and dying relatives for baptism…"

Historian Dave Walter characterized DeSmet as "a stocky, robust bundle of energy." To author Albert Antrei: "[He possessed] a cultured, broad mind, at perfect peace…with itself and in love with its whole world…"

### HISTORIAN LOUIS PFALLER CALLED HIM:

*"the noblest…single character in the long history of Indian and white confrontation in the American West."*

DeSmet inspired converts among most tribes of the Trans-Mississippi West. He negotiated several treaties, most notably with Sitting Bull in 1868. General David Stanley declared: "Father DeSmet alone of the entire white race could penetrate to [the hostile Sioux] and return safe and sound."

Before his death in 1873, DeSmet had crossed the Atlantic nineteen times, visiting popes, kings, and presidents on behalf of American Indians.

*Wallace Street was (and still is) Virginia City's commercial center, but no longer hosts wagons and horse and ox teams.* MONTANA HISTORICAL SOCIETY RESEARCH CENTER PHOTOGRAPH ARCHIVES, HELENA

**May 26, 1863: Bill Fairweather and Henry Edgar struck "pay dirt."** They'd been prospecting along Alder Gulch and set off what historian Mike Malone called "the greatest placer rush of Montana's history."

Edgar recalled: "We staked twelve claims...agree[d] to say nothing of the discovery...prospect the gulch thoroughly and get the best."

At Bannack, they quietly bought provisions, but curious townsfolk got wind of the discovery. Miner Frank Loften declared: "I sure followed them, but so did nearly everybody in town."

### EDGAR'S JOURNAL DESCRIBED THE PANDEMONIUM:

*"Crowds follow after us, they camp right around us, so we can't get away...Such a stampede! I never saw anything like it before."*

Soon a series of makeshift mining camps formed a nearly continuous settlement nicknamed "Fourteen-Mile City" at Alder Gulch. Pioneer F.W. Patten described: "families and messes of men living in houses...wagons...tents...bush arbors, and...under clusters of trees. All are...engaged in searching for and obtaining gold rather than preparing for comfort, or for the approaching winter..."

On June 16, 1863, developers platted the principal town. Southern miners hoped to name the new burg "Varina" in honor of the wife of Confederate president Jefferson Davis. Pro-Union territorial judge G.G. Bissell—a northerner—flatly refused, declaring: "No such blot as this shall stain the honor of the camp." He submitted instead the name "Virginia City."

*Near downtown Virginia City, this cross-street of Wallace held an in-demand blacksmith shop.* Montana Historical Society Research Center Photograph Archives, Helena

**Merchant Alexander Toponce described the mining camps around Virginia City as: "the greatest aggregation of toughs and criminals that ever got together in the west.**

"They came up the Missouri River on steamboats by the scores, deserters from the Union and Rebel armies, river pirates, and professional gamblers…They came by wagon trains from the gold camps of Nevada and California…from the Columbia River country and…from Pike's Peak…"

Congress created Montana Territory on May 26, 1864, exactly a year to the day after the discovery of Alder Gulch gold, and mainly because of it. In 1865, Virginia City became the territorial capital. Ten thousand souls lived there, making it the inland northwest's largest city. Author Gary R. Forney called the boomtown "the epicenter of an amazing confluence of economic, political, social, and cultural forces that would shape Montana's early years."

But new gold discoveries soon drew miners away from Montana's great El Dorado. In the 1870s, an astonished Earl of Dunraven described the deflated Virginia City.

### THE EARL OF DUNRAVEN WROTE:

*"Good Lord!…a street of straggling shanties, a bank, a blacksmith shop, a few dry goods stores, and bar-rooms constitute the main attractions of the 'city'…The whole place was a delusion and a snare."*

Alder Gulch once held the richest placer deposits in Montana. The U.S. Assay Office reported that miners extracted at least $90 million in gold before 1900—in present-day dollars that equals no less than $45 billion.

*For the 1890 edition of Mark Twain's* Roughing It, *an illustrator imagined young Mark Twain (center, wearing sidearm) eagerly interviewing Jack Slade (left) in California, before Slade ever headed to Montana Territory.*

# JACK SLADE

**Jack Slade was Montana's drunken, devilish desperado.**

Virginia City newspaperman Thomas Dimsdale admitted: "From Kearney (Nebraska), west, he was feared a great deal more than the Almighty."

Born in 1829, Joseph Alfred (Jack) Slade committed murder and fled west from Illinois. While working on the Overland Trail, he earned "the reputation of a first class fighting man." During a drunken brawl, stationmaster Jules Reni shot the Slade five times, but Slade escaped. He then returned to torture and kill Reni—removing his ears—which he carried as souvenirs for the rest of his life.

Slade came to Virginia City, Montana, in 1863. When sober, he was a soft-spoken and hard-working gentleman. When drunk, Slade became a bloodthirsty ogre rumored to have killed twenty-six men.

### AUTHOR MARK TWAIN CALLED SLADE:

*"The pitiless scourge of the outlaws, the raw-head-and-bloody-bones the nursing mothers of the mountains terrified their children with."*

The alcoholic Slade terrorized Virginia City—screaming profanities, trashing saloons, and wildly threatening the citizens. After a particularly violent episode, Vigilantes cornered the outlaw, gave him time to write to his wife, then hanged him.

Before the noose went over his head, Slade prayed and wept, lamenting again and again: "My God! My God! Must I die? Oh, my dear wife!"

Newsman Dimsdale pronounced Slade's hanging: "the protest of society on behalf of social order and the rights of man."

*Last Chance Gulch, the crooked, creek-following, main street of Helena, is seen from the south in the 1860s.*

# LAST CHANCE GULCH

**On July 14, 1864, four trail weary and frustrated "Georgians" (actually from Georgia, Alabama, Iowa, and England) made camp at a place they called "Last Chance Gulch."**

Reginald Stanley, the Brit, remembered that they "dug up three or four flat smooth nuggets…that made the pan ring when dropped into it."

Gold seekers flooded into the Gulch.

### PIONEER HENRY BOSE RECALLED:

*"When we got to Last Chance, it certainly was a hell-roaring camp, wild I had never seen the likes before…"*

By 1867, thousands lived in a hodgepodge of dirt-roofed cabins, rough lumber shacks, and raucous hurdy-gurdy houses called Helena. Miners worked every inch of ground. Buildings wound up on stilts as prospectors washed out the promising pay dirt below them.

When Helena became Montana's territorial capital in 1875, its permanence was assured. With the 1883 arrival of a railroad, townsfolk considered their community, as historian Paula Petrik writes, "a bona fide competitor with Denver for the title 'Queen City of the Rockies'."

By 1888, fifty millionaires called Helena home—more per capita than in any other city in the world. Historian Bob Fletcher describes "Cattle kings, mining magnates, merchant princes, and wool tycoons built the mansions…they must have dreamed when they were sleeping in sod-roofed cabins."

Miners extracted $221 million (in today's dollars) from Last Chance Gulch. Even as late as the 1970s, a vein of gold was found under a bank's foundation.

*This drawing of an 1870 bare-knuckle boxing match shows what the Orem-O'Neil fight had looked like five years earlier.*

# OREM-O'NEIL FIGHT

**"One of the longest and most brutal fights in American ring history" was fought in Virginia City, Montana Territory, on January 2, 1865.** *Sports Illustrated* called the 185-round, bare-fisted match: "a grueling display of courage and stamina…"

The contest pitted 29-year-old teetotalling saloonkeeper and veteran welterweight Con Orem against the Irishman Hugh O'Neil, 34, a whiskey-drinking heavyweight.

Fifty-two pounds heavier, O'Neil was a 3-to-1 favorite. Orem's backers trusted his heart and experience. One sportswriter called him: "a quick, wiry bantam rooster of a man…" Historian Warren Brier wrote: "Outside the ring [Con Orem] was a respected citizen…a prosperous businessman. Inside it he was a bundle of venom…"

"A dense crowd clad in as motley style as ever the sun shown upon…" packed J.A. Nelson's Leviathan Hall. They cheered the mismatched gladiators, fighting for a $1,000 purse.

### YOUNG MOLLY SHEEHAN RECALLED:

*"We heard shouts…thuds, grunts, and heavy breathing—a melee of sounds… Two men, all but stripped…were pummeling each other furiously, brutally. Crowds of men surged about in seething excitement."*

Ninety-one falls punctuated the slugfest that lasted more than three hours. Finally the referee shouted: "The fight is over. It's a draw. All bets are off."

The underdog, Con Orem, had battled to a stalemate and retained his title as "the unofficial champion of the Rocky Mountains."

*The sole known image of John Bozeman, who died at age thirty-two.*

# JOHN BOZEMAN'S TRAIL

**Indians and trappers had long followed a route north from the Powder River Basin.** But when gold-seekers used it as a shortcut to Montana's mining camps, it got its name—the "Bloody Bozeman."

Traveler W.J. Davies called John Bozeman "brave" and "determined[,]…a man the people would [readily] follow almost anywhere." In the summer of 1863, Bozeman began piloting wagon trains north from the Oregon Trail to Virginia City. By 1866, more than 3500 people had made the three-month, 500-mile journey.

But Bozeman's trail cut right through the last great hunting grounds of the Northern Plains Indians, violating the Fort Laramie Treaty of 1851. Tension escalated.

The Lakota warrior Red Cloud protested: "The Great Father sends us presents and wants a new road, [but then] goes with soldiers to steal road before Indian says yes or no!"

## YOUNG-MAN-AFRAID-OF-HIS-HORSES WARNED:

### *"In two moons you will not have a hoof left!"*

Black Elk, the Lakota holy man, recalled: "It [was] like some fearful thing in a fog…[E]veryone was saying that [the white men] were coming…to take our country and rub us all out, and that we should all have to die fighting."

Indian attacks along the trail were frequent. The army built forts to protect the route. On December 21, 1866, two thousand Sioux and Cheyenne warriors annihilated Captain William J. Fetterman and eighty men. Indian warriors had never inflicted a worse defeat on the U.S. Army.

Within a year, the Army had abandoned three forts, and civilian travel ended along "the last great overland…trail in the American West."

*Red Cloud was a mature Oglala Sioux leader in the 1860s and 1870s, who first tried warfare then turned to diplomacy to save his people's traditional ways.*

# RED CLOUD

**Red Cloud was "the warrior-statesman of the Oglala Sioux."** Born about 1821, he waged "the most successful war against the United States ever fought by an Indian nation."

Red Cloud led the native resistance to the Bozeman Trail—a wagon road through eastern Wyoming to the Montana gold fields. Historian J. Jay Myers declared: "[He] was the only Plains Indian who could gather so many confederates and keep them together long enough to wage a successful campaign against the white man…"

Between 1866 and 1868, Red Cloud's warriors repeatedly attacked wagon trains and forts in an ugly guerrilla war along the "bloody Bozeman." More than seventy overland travelers died. Red Cloud's troops also annihilated the entire 82-man command of Colonel William Fetterman, just outside Fort Phil Kearny, Wyoming.

### PHOTOGRAPHER WILLIAM HENRY JACKSON DESCRIBED RED CLOUD AS:

*"Six feet in height and straight as an arrow; his face…indicative of indomitable courage…and his full, piercing eyes seem to take in at a glance the character of friend or foe."*

Red Cloud brokered the Fort Laramie Treaty of 1868. The agreement closed the Bozeman Trail forts and temporarily guaranteed the Lakota possession of the Black Hills.

When Red Cloud died in 1909, the *New York Times* dubbed him "a man of brains, a good ruler, an eloquent speaker, an able general, and fair diplomat."

*Missionary extraordinaire, "Brother Van" ministered to people's mundane needs as well as their spiritual ones.*

# BROTHER VAN

**The Blackfeet called William Wesley Van Orsdel—Montana's beloved pioneer circuit preacher—"Great Heart."** Most whites knew him simply as "Brother Van."

Methodist Bishop Cooke described him as a "strong soul, like the mountains, rock-ribbed in moral strength—his very presence said 'Here's a man!' And yet he was as kind and gentle and beautiful in his unconscious demeanor as a little child."

Brother Van arrived in Montana in 1872 and soon became a missionary at large. During the next five decades he preached across the Treasure State, creating converts wherever he went.

One old-timer recalled: "Everybody knew that if Brother Van came to visit…he would pitch in to cleaning the barn, milking the cow, cutting wood, churning butter, rocking the baby, or any other job that needed to be done."

Van Orsdel motivated Montanans to build a hundred small churches and fifty homes for their pastors. He helped construct seven Deaconess Hospitals, a nurse's home, the Intermountain Children's Home, and Montana Wesleyan University (now Rocky Mountain College).

UPON VAN ORSDEL'S DEATH IN 1919,
BISHOP COOKE SUMMED UP THE UNIVERSAL
ESTIMATE OF THE MINISTER'S CHARACTER:

*"Brother Van was everybody's friend. I don't believe that there was a dog in the state that would not wag his tail when he saw him coming…If you want to see his monument, look around."*

*Yankee Jim's cabin in Montana, just north of Yellowstone National Park, today is preserved by the U.S. government.*

# YANKEE JIM

**Ohioan James George—better known as Yankee Jim—came to Montana in 1863. In his words, he "left home on the toe of his father's boot."**

In 1873, Yankee Jim built the National Park Toll Road—a crude, gated artery through the narrow canyon between Paradise Valley and Yellowstone Park. *The Rocky Mountain American* observed: "Yankee Jim was ruthless in exacting the tribute…But…he was equally royal as a gracious host."

A Park County sheriff remarked: "He puts in an average of about five days lapping up corn juice and telling the whoppingest lies ever incubated on the Yellowstone and [then] ten days of neutralizing the effects of them by talking…religion."

Yankee Jim was furious when the Northern Pacific Railroad ended his toll road monopoly in 1883.

### NEIGHBOR GAY RANDALL RECALLED:

*"Every day when [he] heard the train coming he would rush out, his long snow-white…beard waving in the breeze, and with his bony hands clinched into fists fling…cuss words from a seemingly inexhaustible vocabulary of profane language."*

Yankee Jim entertained thousands of tourists, from poet Rudyard Kipling to President Teddy Roosevelt. He declared: "People from all over the world have stopped at my place—millionaires, royal dukes, lords and presidents…I don't have a fancy house, but they come to see me anyway."

*The name of some Indians of the Columbia Plateau—or of small and tough Indian ponies in general—now is spelled "cayuse," but the "Kiyus" saloon nonetheless made it through the Great Helena Fire of 1874.*

# GREAT HELENA FIRE OF 1874

**Montana's greatest gold camp, Helena, was built to burn.** It was crowded, with tinder-dry log and frame buildings, water was scarce, and its funnel-like main street acted like "a natural chimney."

And burn it did: from 1869 through 1874, nine fires roared through Helena—three completely gutted the city's business district. Typical headlines read: "This poor, afflicted, unfortunate city has been visited by another destructive conflagration."

The Great Helena Fire of 1874 was called "The Blaze of the Century." It started accidentally in a Chinese gambling house. The *Memphis Daily Appeal* wrote: "A heavy wind blowing at the time directly toward the heart of the city, the flames soon spread over the whole town and, despite the heroic efforts of firemen and citizens[,] jumped Bridge Street, thence down both sides of Main Street…" The *Los Angeles Daily Herald* reported: "At one time it was thought the whole town would be laid into ashes."

And racial tensions exploded.

THE *HELENA INDEPENDENT* NOTED:

*"Feeling ran high against the Chinese…and residents armed with six-shooters cowed most of the Orientals and made them man the big pump."*

The fire killed only one person, but it destroyed 150 homes, the Montana Historical Society's archives, and most of the town's businesses. Property losses totaled one million dollars.

But as before, "the Queen City of the Rockies" rebuilt quickly. Just one year after the Great Fire, Montanans named Helena their new territorial capital.

Frank Leslie's Illustrated Newspaper *featured this artist's conception of a Sioux charge during the Battle of the Rosebud.*

# BATTLE OF THE ROSEBUD (PART 1)

**In June 1876, on the plains of eastern Montana Territory, the infamous Indian fighter General George Crook** and 1,300 troops, including 261 Crow and Shoshoni scouts, clashed with 1,500 Sioux, Cheyenne, and Arapaho that included inspiring warrior Crazy Horse. The Battle of the Rosebud became a ferocious six-hour fight.

Crook's aide-de-camp, Captain Azor Nickerson, described the conflict's opening moments: "Every hill appeared to be covered with…swarming legions [of Sioux and Cheyenne]…Many wore the long…warbonnet of eagle plumes, which…fluttered in the air, back of the wearer, to the distance of 5 or 6 feet, while others wore half masks of the heads of wild animals, with the ears and sometimes the horns still protruding, giving them the appearance of devils from the netherworld…"

## A SOLDIER RECALLED:

*"They were in front, rear, flanks, and on every hilltop far and near. I had been in several Indian battles, but never saw so many Indians at one time before… or so brave."*

The *New York Daily Graphic's* eyewitness account reported: "The firing was … terrific…Officers who were through the [Civil] war…say that they never in their experience saw anything hotter…[T]he Sioux advanced… urging their ponies to their utmost speed…Men brave and true, were falling every moment…The line…growing thinner and thinner, seemed to be dwindling so constantly that annihilation was apparently but a question of time…"

The Battle of the Rosebud was fought just eight days before and a few dozen miles from the Battle of the Little Big Horn.

*As a military man, Captain Anson Mills was stunned by Northern Cheyenne warriors' tactics while he fought them in the Battle of the Rosebud.*

# BATTLE OF THE ROSEBUD (PART 2)

**In 1874, trespassing miners discovered gold in the Black Hills of South Dakota.** The U.S. wanted the land, but the Lakota and Cheyenne people refused. The result was the Battle of the Rosebud in June 1876.

The Northern Cheyenne warrior Wooden Leg recalled: "Until the sun went far toward the west there were charges back and forth. Our Indians fought and ran away...The soldiers and their Indian scouts did the same. Sometimes we chased them, sometimes they chased us."

### CAPTAIN ANSON MILLS LATER WROTE:

*"The Indians proved...that they were the best cavalry soldiers on earth. In charging... they exposed little of their persons...firing and lancing from underneath the horses' necks, so that there was no part on the Indian at which we could aim."*

The *Cincinnati Enquirer* reported: "The Sioux, all well mounted and well armed...were prodigal in the use of ammunition..." Crook's troops fired an estimated 25,000 rounds that day.

Finally, out of ammo, with supply wagons far to the rear, Crook retreated to Wyoming. History will never know if his force could have arrived in time to save Custer's command at the Battle of the Little Big Horn eight days later.

Crook reported losses of thirty-two killed and twenty-one wounded. Estimates for Indian losses were a dozen killed and twenty wounded. The Rosebud battlefield, near Busby, is now a Montana state park.

*Gall sat for photographer David F. Barry in 1881.*

# GALL

**Gall was the Lakota war chief U.S. Army soldier's dubbed "the Fighting Cock of the Sioux."**

Historian Charles Eastman called him "one of the most aggressive leaders of the Sioux nation in their last stand for freedom."

To Indian agent James McLaughlin, Gall was "a large man of noble presence with military talents of high order..." Libbie Custer, wife of the slain general, called Gall "the finest specimen of a warrior" she had ever seen.

Gall was uncompromising. At an 1868 Treaty Conference he stated bluntly: "The whites ruin our country...The military posts on the Missouri River must be removed and the steamboats stopped from coming here."

Fearless, Gall wore a conspicuous red blanket in combat. He was Sitting Bull's ace-in-the-hole at the Battle of the Little Big Horn.

### AUTHOR JAMES WELCH WROTE THAT GALL:

*"Fought the longest and hardest of any warrior that day [but he] also lost the most."*

Gall saw two wives and three children cut down by Major Reno's detachment. He later recalled: "It made my heart bad...After that I killed all my enemies with the hatchet."

Following Custer's defeat, Gall lived in Canada before finally returning to Montana to surrender in 1881. When "Buffalo Bill" Cody sought to obtain Gall as one of his Wild West Show's leading attractions, Gall flatly refused, declaring: "I am not an animal to be exhibited before the crowd."

He died at Oak Creek, South Dakota, in 1894.

*Curly was photographed a few months after reporting the Battle of the Little Bighorn.*

# CURLY

**Two days after the 1876 Battle of the Little Big Horn, a terrified seventeen-year-old Crow scout named Curly approached General Alfred Terry's headquarters.**

Curly brought news of Custer's defeat—the first news to reach the outside world.

Curly, using sign language, disclosed the story of Custer's doomed command. He later admitted: "I did nothing wonderful—I was not in the fight."

In time, however, Curly began billing himself as the "sole survivor of Custer's massacre." Curly's claims included: crawling to safety as the battle raged, cowering under a Sioux blanket, hiding within a disemboweled horse, even trying to persuade a gallant Custer to retreat.

Historian Steven Conliff wrote: "Curly became a skilled 'raconteur'...continually...embellishing his original story."

The scout became a celebrity. Historians, newspapermen, Hollywood producers, and tourists flocked to hear his frequently self-glorifying tales.

### THE *BILLINGS GAZETTE* CALLED CURLY:

*"Probably the most photographed Indian in America."*

During the battle's tenth anniversary, Gall—the great Lakota warrior—confronted Curly, publicly charging: "You were a coward and ran away before the battle began." Later, he demanded to see Curly's wings because: "nothing but a bird could have escaped after we surrounded the whites."

Curly died in 1924 near Crow Agency. Mystery still surrounds his exact role at Custer's defeat.

*Libbie Bacon Custer*

# LIBBIE CUSTER

**Elizabeth Bacon "Libbie" Custer was the wife of "the boy general with the golden locks," George Armstrong Custer.**

Though petite and refined, Libbie Custer, as the *New York Times* reported, "trod the unfrequented path for a woman of open campaigning" through Civil War battles and Plain Indian conflicts. To Mrs. Custer, it was better to "face the dangers of the wilds than the sorrow of being left behind."

### THE *NEW YORK TIMES* WROTE:

*"[S]he slept where she could, drank water that in her own words contained 'natural History,' and never dared confess to a headache, depression or fatigue."*

The day her headstrong husband and his entire regiment rode away towards their deaths in eastern Montana, she experienced "a premonition of disaster that I had never known before weighed me down...I shut into my heart the most uncontrollable anxiety..."

After the Little Big Horn disaster, President Ulysses S. Grant and much of the press blamed Custer. Though nearly penniless from her husband's unpublicized gambling habit, Libbie fought back with a half-century-long, one-woman campaign to portray her man as the gallant fallen hero of "Custer's Last Stand." She wrote three popular books glorifying his memory, lectured across the country, and lobbied in Washington to create a national monument in Montana. Almost single-handedly she secured his iconic legacy.

Libbie Custer never visited the site of Montana's most famous battle, stating she'd be unable to "suppress the emotions that...the place would surely call forth." She died at age ninety-one in New York City and was buried at West Point beside her husband.

*Miles posed in the clothing that earned his Indian nickname of "Bear Coat."*
MONTANA HISTORICAL SOCIETY RESEARCH CENTER PHOTOGRAPH ARCHIVES, HELENA

**Montana's greatest Indian fighter was arguably General Nelson Miles.** But his wife's uncle, General William Tecumseh Sherman, once admitted: "I know of no way to satisfy his ambitions but to surrender to him absolute power over the whole Army, with President and Congress thrown in."

### HISTORIAN ELLIOT WEST CALLED HIM:

*"[A] preening chest puffer, relentlessly and insufferably self-serving."*

Miles earned a Congressional Medal of Honor in the Civil War, then was assigned to fight Indians in the Red River area before being sent to Montana after the Custer debacle. Miles believed: "going to meet the enemies of civilization…was a delightful enterprise."

General Miles' men built Fort Keogh and were in regular pursuit of the Indians. Author Michael Punke wrote: "[Miles] fit the total warfare policy like a sword to its scabbard."

Miles waged "the severest of winter campaigns" in 1876-1877 against thousands of non-reservation Lakota Sioux and Northern Cheyenne. In January 1877, his troops clashed with Two Moon's warriors at the Battle of Wolf Mountain. The army seized hundreds of horses, tipis, and most of the Sioux food supply. That October, Miles intercepted Chief Joseph's Nez Perce forty miles from Canada. Years later, assigned to the Southwest, Miles accepted Geronimo's surrender.

Miles boasted: "I…have fought and defeated larger and better armed bodies of hostile Indians than any other officer since the history of Indian warfare commenced."

Miles eventually became Commanding General of the Army. Montana's Miles City bears his name.

*Yellowstone Kelly in his frontier gear.*

# LUTHER "YELLOWSTONE" KELLY

**"Yellowstone" Kelly's scouting abilities equaled Kit Carson's and Daniel Boone's.** Buffalo Bill Cody called him a "good man to tie to."

Luther Sage Kelly was born in upstate New York in 1849. As a teenager, he rambled westward, journeying—as he later recalled—wherever the "spirit of adventure might lead me, until I had reached the wild country at the headwaters of the Missouri."

Kelly dressed the part of a fearless frontiersman—sporting a full mustache, shoulder length, raven-black hair, animal skins, and beaded moccasins. He kept his Henry repeating rifle—affectionately dubbed "Old Sweetness"—encased in the skin of a giant bull snake.

But unlike most of his peers, Kelly was an educated man, fond of reading Edgar Allan Poe, Sir Walter Scott, and William Shakespeare.

## BIOGRAPHER JERRY KEENAN DUBBED HIM:

*"A handsome, buckskin-clad, straight shootin', poetry-spouting frontiersman..."*

As chief scout for General Nelson Miles, Kelly tracked Indians for the U.S. Army. Miles proclaimed him "one of the most intelligent frontiersmen and explorers in our service."

Kelly befriended Teddy Roosevelt, guided Alaskan expeditions, fought in the Philippines during the Spanish-American War, and administered to Apaches as an Indian agent.

Shortly before his death in 1938, Kelly wrote: "I feel my body will better rest in Montana...than in the vastness of Arlington."

He was buried with full military honors on a bluff overlooking the Yellowstone Valley.

*An artist in 1877 showed American readers his interpretation of the army's attack in the Big Hole.*

# BATTLE OF THE BIG HOLE

**Before dawn on August 9, 1877, Colonel John Gibbon and nearly two hundred troops attacked Chief Joseph's Nez Perce encampment on the Big Hole River in southwestern Montana.** His orders: no prisoners, no negotiations.

Soldiers rushed the village, shooting indiscriminately into tipis. The warrior Young White Bird recalled: "Bullets were like hail on the camp…" One lieutenant remembered: "the ground…covered with the dead and dying, the morning air laden with smoke and riven by cheers, savage yells, shrieks, curses and groans." Corporal Charles Loynes saw a baby at a dead woman's breast, "crying as it swung its little arm back and forth—the lifeless hand flapping at the wrist broken by a bullet."

The survivors scattered. But as the soldiers paused to burn the camp, the Nez Perce regrouped.

## WHITE BIRD SHOUTED:

*"Are we going to run…to let the whites kill our women and children before our eyes? It is better we should be killed fighting. Now is our time. Fight!"*

Advancing Indians took rifles from fallen troops, pressed hard, and returned fire. More soldiers fell. Badly wounded, his horse crippled, Colonel Gibbon realized his "untenable position" and retreated.

Yellow Wolf described the aftermath: "Wounded children screaming with pain. Women and men wailing for their scattered dead. The air…heavy with sorrow…"

Ninety Nez Perce and thirty-one whites died at the Battle of the Big Hole. Historian Aubrey Haines called it: "similar to a Greek tragedy—quite devoid of real winners, from any viewpoint."

*Little Wolf stands beside Dull Knife.*

# LITTLE WOLF

**The naturalist and Indian scholar George Bird Grinnell called Little Wolf "the greatest Indian I have ever known."**

Little Wolf was a powerful nineteenth-century chief, and the leader of the NorthernCheyenne exodus from Oklahoma.

After the Battle of the Little Big Horn, the U.S. Army forcibly relocated the Northern Cheyenne south to Indian Territory. Disease and starvation were rampant. Little Wolf complained: "We are sickly and dying here… no one will speak our names when we are dead."

September 10, 1878: Little Wolf, Dull Knife, and 336 women and children start a 1500-mile freedom flight to Montana. Traveling by moonlight, hiding in broken timber, they evaded 2,000 pursuing soldiers.

The going is hard. Dozens died. Dull Knife's weaker band surrenders in Nebraska. But Little Wolf and 113 others press on to Montana.

### AT FORT KEOGH, LITTLE WOLF EXPLAINED:

*"Our hearts…longed for this country where we were born. There are only a few of us left, and we only wanted a little ground where we could live."*

In 1884, the Northern Cheyenne secured a reservation on the Tongue River. Little Wolf lived there until his death in 1904.

Northern Cheyenne President Eugene Little Coyote honored him in 2007 with these words: "We have a homeland because of his leadership…We want to remember…because if that didn't happen, we might not have a reservation today, we might not have a tribe."

*L.A. Huffman in 1926*

**Laton Alton Huffman was the "pioneer photographer of Miles City."**

Biographers Mark Brown and W.R. Felton maintained: "No other photographer captured pictorially the true western frontier…with such sensitive authenticity as did this now widely acclaimed genius…"

Born in 1854, Huffman became post photographer at Fort Keogh at age twenty-five. He recalled: "This Yellowstone-Big Horn country was then unpenned of wire, and unspoiled by railway…Eastman had not yet made the Kodak but…I made photographs. With crude, home-made cameras, from saddle and in log shack, I saved something…"

The great chiefs, the soldiers, the buffalo hunters, the cowboys, the townsfolk—Huffman preserved all their images on glass plate negatives.

Huffman travelled the range on horseback—lugging a 50-pound camera, four-legged tripod, and deadly chemicals. His prints, postcards, and hand-colored photographs provide us with an unvarnished visual record of early Montana and inspired western artists like Frederick Remington and Charlie Russell.

### THE *RONAN PIONEER* REPORTED:

*"With Huffman, photography has been…a labor of love. He would rather make a good picture than eat a square meal…"*

Historian J. Evetts Haley wrote: "…the frontier opened to L.A. Huffman its closing but most colorful pages…Huffman sensed the significance of what he saw and set himself the honest job or recording it in detail…"

In 1976, Huffman became the only photographer ever inducted into the National Cowboy Hall of Fame.

*Dressed for a formal portrait, Yellowstone Vic Smith looks little like his buffalo-shooting frontier persona.* MONTANA HISTORICAL SOCIETY RESEARCH CENTER PHOTOGRAPH ARCHIVES, HELENA

# YELLOWSTONE VIC SMITH AND THE BUFFALO SLAUGHTER

**Montana's "champion buffalo hunter" was Yellowstone Vic Smith.**

Smith rubbed elbows with George Custer, Liver Eatin' Johnson, and Sitting Bull. But it was during Montana's Indian wars, as a government-sponsored buffalo hunter, that he became a legend.

Teddy Roosevelt praised "Old Vic" as "the best hunter in the West," noting, "he can cut the head off a…grouse at…100 yards …"

Smith practiced constantly—some claimed he shot at least 20,000 cartridges a day. During the winter of 1881, he single-handedly killed more than 5,000 buffalo on Montana's Little Missouri and Yellowstone rivers. As Smith said: "When we got through [with] the hunt there was not a hoof left."

General Philip Sheridan praised Smith and his cohorts. "These men have done more…to settle the vexed Indian question, than the entire regular army has done in the last forty years. They are destroying the Indians' commissary… [L]et them kill, skin, and sell until the buffaloes are exterminated. Then your prairies can be covered with speckled cattle."

Smith later confessed: "If a man made such killings now, he would be dubbed a game hog…But in those days, when there were millions of buffalo…a dead shot was looked up to…the same as any hero of the present day."

## IN HIS MEMOIRS, SMITH WISHED:

### *"My aim hadn't been so good."*

Smith wrote: "How easily our government could have extended a protecting hand and saved those noble animals from almost utter extinction."

*The 1880 Crow delegation to Washington included, front row left to right, Medicine Crow, Plenty Coups, Pretty Eagle, Long Elk, and Old Crow. Back row, Crow agent A.M. Quivey, Two Belly, agent A.R. Keller, interpreter Thomas Stewart.*

# CROW INDIAN RAILROAD NEGOTIATIONS

**Most Crow Indians wanted no part of the Northern Pacific Railroad.** Indian Agent A.R. Keller, warned his superiors: "The Reservation [belongs to] the Indians, guaranteed…by solemn treaty…They do not wish to part with it, and will not do so unless through force or fear, or being badgered into it."

Following Keller's report, President Rutherford B. Hayes transported Crow leaders to the nation's capital for some executive arm-twisting. He vowed to build each Crow family a house and barn, and to educate Crow children—all for a railroad right-of-way across the Yellowstone Valley.

Chief Plenty Coups recalled: "the President kept us in Washington for over a month. We had several conferences…[He] tried to overrule our objections, but he failed."

Pretty Eagle said: "The whites got together and talked until it made my heart feel dead…I…told [the great Father] that I would not let…the railroad, pass over my land…Finally [he] told us…that if we did not give it up it might be bad for us, that they might put us in some other place."

The Crow leaders returned to Montana to confer with their people.

### CHIEF MEDICINE CROW ADVISED:

*"If we say yes, the whites will bring the railroad across our land…If we say no, the whites will bring it just the same. We had better say yes."*

In 1882 the Crow tribe reluctantly agreed to reduce their reservation by 1.5 million acres and grant access to the Northern Pacific Railroad.

*The Portland-bound "gold spike train" stops at Gold Creek, Montana, for the Northern Pacific's ceremonial completion.* Montana Historical Society Research Center Photograph Archives, Helena

# THE FINAL SPIKE ON THE NORTHERN PACIFIC

**On September 8, 1883, "a motley gathering" of nearly three thousand assembled in remote Gold Creek, southeast of Missoula.**

A *New York Times* reporter saw: "newspapermen[,]...artists making sketches, photographers setting up their tripods and cameras, miners, herdsmen, ranchers, orators, Indians, smug business men, women with crying babies, English noblemen, foreign diplomats, railroad laborers and officials, negro servants, and United States...Congressmen all higgledy-piggledy."

All had come to witness history—the completion of the Northern Pacific Railway linking the Great Lakes and Washington's Puget Sound.

Former President Ulysses S. Grant and other dignitaries made speeches. Then the audience crowded along the rail-bed. German journalist Paul Lindau described the scene: "Workers began an impassioned race to complete the last mile—Caucasians from the east, Chinese from the west...Rails slammed onto ties, taking their places as if by magic and were fastened with spikes hit in a violent rat-a-tat-tat."

### JOURNALIST LINDAU WROTE:

*"Suddenly a wild feverish howl! Breathless and bathed in sweat, sunburned and dusty fellows reached the goal and screamed and yelled and waved their hats... The job was done."*

NP president Henry Villard drove the final spike, completing the transcontinental railroad that, in the words of the *Portland Oregonian*, "[had] annihilated time and space..."

*Above: Even in black and white, Abbott's brilliantly blue eyes showed; he was 18 at the time.*

*Right: One day at a saloon in Gilt Edge, Calamity Jane and Teddy Blue stepped outdoors and exchanged hats for the camera.*

# "TEDDY BLUE" ABBOTT

**Montana seldom saw a range rider as colorful as "Teddy Blue" Abbott.**

Born in England, Edward Charles Abbott came to the United States in 1871. At just ten years old, he helped drive a herd of Texas cattle to Nebraska. He said it "made a cowboy out of me. Nothing could have changed me after that."

Abbott recalled: "The [cattle]...run wild while the men was away fighting [the Civil War]...Here was all these cheap, long-horned steers overrunning Texas; here was the rest of the country crying for beef—and no railroads to get them out. So they trailed them out...From that time on the big drives were made every year, and the cowboy was born..."

During the open-range heyday, Abbott drove longhorns north from Texas to Montana. In his 1930s memoir, *We Pointed Them North*, he described stampedes, vicious 50-degree-below-zero snowstorms, and getting knocked off his horse by lightning twice.

### BIOGRAPHER HELENA HUNTINGTON SMITH DESCRIBED ABBOTT AS:

*"Tough as whipcord...and boiling with energy...[He] was the history of the cattle trail and the open range."*

Abbott later settled down to raise a family on a ranch near Lewistown. Summing up his colorful life he said: "Only a few of us are left now and they are scattered from Texas to Canada. The rest...have gone ahead across the big divide...I hope they find good water and plenty of grass. But wherever they are is where I want to go."

*Nannie Alderson (1860-1947), in her later years, showed both the hard-working life she'd lived and the optimism that got her through it.* MONTANA HISTORICAL SOCIETY RESEARCH CENTER PHOTOGRAPH ARCHIVES, HELENA

# NANNIE ALDERSON

**Nannie Alderson and her husband, Walt, rode the railcars to Miles City in 1883.** The newlyweds homesteaded on Lame Deer Creek, hoping to quickly capitalize on the beef bonanza, and then return east.

In her memoir, *A Bride Goes West*, Alderson recalled: "[At first] we didn't mind the hard things because we didn't expect them to last. Montana… was booming…and the same feverish optimism possessed all of us…It… looked so easy…and we could figure it all out…how in no time at all we'd all be cattle kings."

Alderson's hopes soon faded. In the spring of 1884—the very day her first baby was born—Northern Cheyenne warriors burned the Alderson cabin as punishment for the couple's unwittingly trespassing on reservation lands. Alderson recalled it was then that she "began to pioneer in earnest…no longer borne up by the belief that our trials were temporary."

The Aldersons relocated to the Tongue River. Those years were, in Nannie's words, "the hardest of my life…for…I had nothing…to cling to…."

## ALDERSON WROTE:

*"You had to keep up or go under—and keeping up made such hard work."*

Ten years after coming west to get rich, the Aldersons abandoned ranching and moved to Miles City.

Summing up the Aldersons' travails, and those of their hardy contemporaries, author William Bevis observed: "It was a beginning for Montana, that finally rewarded, not…dreams of open space where 'a poor man can grow rich,' but endurance."

*Tommy Cruse, who never learned to read or to write more than his name, seems to have avoided sitting for the camera as well. The Maskelyne Tunnel was one entrance to his fabled Drumlummon Mine.*

# THE CRUSE-CARTER WEDDING

**Irishman Thomas "Tommy" Cruse discovered a rich ledge of gold in his Drumlummon Mine near Marysville in 1876.** A few years later he was Montana's "Millionaire Miner."

In 1886, the fifty-year-old prospector proposed to Maggie Carter, age twenty-three, a dressmaker described as "a faithful maiden of modest, retiring disposition."

Bishop John Brondel married the happy couple on a snow-covered March morning in Helena. It was the "wedding of the century."

Historian Ellen Baumler wrote: "To the merry chime of sleigh bells, 'large throngs of people...moved with common impulse' toward the Cathedral of the Sacred Hearts...The scent of orange blossoms and other exotic blooms ...shipped from as far away as Portland and St. Paul, perfumed the frosty air..."

The *Washington Critic* called their reception "the most brilliant affair known in the territory." Courts adjourned. Businesses closed. Banners flew. Two thousand well-wishers flocked to the city.

### THE *OMAHA DAILY BEE* REPORTED:

*"The whole town went on a spree for a week...wine in galore, edibles of every description, and pure, unalloyed joyfulness..."*

Cruse picked up the gigantic tab without blinking an eye, then presented his blushing bride with a wedding gift—a check for $500,000.

But just ten months later—tragedy: Maggie Carter Cruse died in childbirth. Journalists mused: "comfort and ...joy...left [Helena's 'Bonanza King'] ...without hope or spirit to battle with the world anew..."

*Chief Plenty Coups, standing second from left, came to oversee treatment of warriors who surrendered after Sword Bearer's Uprising. Whoever numbered this photograph wrongfully assumed he was one of the rebels.* NATIONAL AR-CHIVES AND RECORDS ADMINISTRATION, ARC IDENTIFIER 531126

# SWORD BEARER'S UPRISING

**Sword Bearer gathered a group of mostly teenaged followers willing to fight white rule on the normally peaceful Crow Reservation in 1887.**

Soldiers were called in. Sword Bearer sent runners to neighboring reservations in a failed attempt to drum up support for a multi-tribal revolt. Seeking peace, the Crow leader Pretty Eagle declared: "[Sword Bearer] is a great Man ...all things bend before him... [but] the Crows do not want to fight."

Sword Bearer refused to turn himself in. General Thomas Ruger issued an ultimatum. Most of the tribe took cover, but Sword Bearer and 150 warriors readied themselves for the last Indian battle fought in Montana.

## ONE EYEWITNESS RECALLED:

*"...wearing his war bonnet of...trailing eagle feathers...[Sword Bearer] came at a gallop...calling and singing, and throwing his red sword into the air, catching it by the hilt as it fell."*

The *New York Times* reported that a "red hot skirmish" followed. Shots were fired. One bluecoat and seven Crow warriors fell. A dozen more were wounded. When Sword Bearer scrambled to escape, an Indian policeman shot him in the head. Headlines in Miles City's *Daily Yellowstone Journal* callously declared: "Sword Bearer...is a Good Indian Now."

Historian Frederick Hoxie concluded: "Sword Bearer represented a brief moment in Crow defiance...[which] typified the common opposition all Plains Indians felt to the 'slavery' of reservation life."

*Pierre Wibaux's statue in his namesake town overlooks his empire.*

# PIERRE WIBAUX

**Pierre Wibaux was "the millionaire cattle king of eastern Montana."**

According to journalist "Montana Lou" Grill: "He persevered under…all conditions and reached that lofty pinnacle…where he was king of all… He was at one time the individual owner of more head of cattle than any other person in the United States."

In 1883, at age twenty-five, Wibaux spurned his life of luxury in France and immigrated to Montana's "bad lands." He settled near Mingusville—a town author Eric Thane called: "a lurid dive, reputed to be one of the hell-holes of creation…"

Wibaux later recalled: "Neighbors were few and far between, and we had the whole country to range in…I picked out what I considered…the finest natural location for a ranch…and since then I…have never seen a better one."

After the Hard Winter of 1886-1887, Wibaux bought up bovine survivors of nearby open range cattle outfits at bargain basement prices. His herd grew to more than 65,000 head.

### WRITING HIS BROTHER, WIBAUX ASSERTED:

*"You can't imagine this country from a business point of view…Only the lazy and stupid fellows remain poor here."*

Wibaux convinced the Northern Pacific Railroad to build a stockyard and bring rail services to Mingusville. By 1895, when the boomtown was re-named Wibaux, it had become what author Joseph Kinsey Howard called: "the greatest livestock…shipping point in the west."

*The quiet—but still threatening—side of Cantrell.* MONTANA HISTORICAL SOCIETY RESEARCH CENTER PHOTOGRAPH ARCHIVES, HELENA

# FLOPPIN' BILL CANTRELL

**William "Floppin' Bill" Cantrell was the bane of all cattle rustlers.**

Journalist W.W. Cheely wrote: "[T]here wasn't a man in the entire country that could hold a candle to him in daring or recklessness...his name was feared...by every horse thief and outlaw in central and northern Montana."

Cantrell earned his nickname as a Missouri River woodchopper, boasting that with just one, Paul Bunyan-style axe swing, cottonwoods just flopped over, stacked and ready to fuel the next passing steamboat.

### AN ACQUAINTANCE SAID:

*"Floppin' Bill took the cake. He was...a perfect devil...He would fight at the drop of a hat—and drop that hat himself."*

When horse thieves stole Cantrell's livestock and kidnapped his Assiniboine wife, historian Dave Walter wrote, the man "became maniacal." Floppin' Bill's gang hunted and eventually lynched nine rustlers. He likely shot and killed another ten or twelve "before they could be decently hanged."

Cantrell then led a rustler roundup from the mouth of the Yellowstone to the Canadian line. An estimated sixty horse thieves were killed during his bloody spree. The *New York Times* reported: "Flopping Bill and his party...are making the lives of the horse-stealing fraternity of the upper country a wild and terrible uncertainty."

The *Billings Gazette* later recalled: "raft building [became] popular and many a man...saved his neck by floating down to Saint Louis."

In 1901, an oncoming locomotive killed Floppin' Bill when his foot caught in the tracks of a Kansas City rail yard.

*James J. Hill, late in a productive life*

# JAMES J. HILL

**James J. Hill was a scrappy, hot-tempered Canadian nick-named "the empire builder."**

Historian Stewart Holbrook characterized Hill as: "the barbed-wire, shaggy headed, one-eyed old son-of-a-bitch of Western railroading."

Hill sensed that Montana's abundant resources could support a second transcontinental line—the Great Northern Railway. Hill's 9,000 workers invaded Montana territory on June 13, 1887. Covering as many as seven miles a day, they raced up the Missouri and Milk River valleys.

Writer Charles Dudley Warner gushed: "Those who saw this army of men and teams stretching over the prairies and casting up this continental highway think they beheld one of the most striking achievements of civilization."

### HILL BRAGGED:

*"Give me enough Swedes and whiskey and I'll build a railroad through hell!"*

By November, Hill's crew had reached Helena, and laid 643 continuous miles of track in just seven and a half months. By 1893, the Great Northern had linked Saint Paul to Seattle. No railroad had ever been built so rapidly.

Historian Mike Malone described the Great Northern as: "one of the best constructed and most profitable of the world's major railroads." It was the first transcontinental built without public money, and one of the few to never go bankrupt.

"When we are all dead and gone," Hill once said, "the sun will still shine, the rain will fall, and this railroad will run as usual."

*Sheet music of the era spread sentimental reactions to tragedies like the Blizzard of 1888.*

# BLIZZARD OF 1888

**In January 1888 a giant blizzard stretched from Montana to Lake Michigan**—the *Great Falls Tribune* called it "the worst [storm] ever known in the northwest…" It was only a year after the Hard Winter of 1886-1887 ended the open range.

Author David Laskin described the 1888 storm: "The air grew still for a long, eerie measure, then the sky began to roar and a wall of ice dust blasted the prairie. Every crevice, every gap…instantly filled with shattered crystals, blinding, smothering, suffocating, burying anything exposed to the wind."

The *New Zealand Herald* wrote: "The air was full of snow as fine as flour…and the darkness caused by so much snow in the air made the scene the most dismal, drear, and forsaken that man ever looked upon."

## MONTANA HEADLINES PROCLAIMED:
### *"Ice King Enthroned."*

Five-foot drifts stalled trains, obliterated roads and downed telegraph lines. The *New York Times* reported: "The whole open country is one vast upheaved ocean, as if the white caps had frozen solid, and the rough waves, snow-covered, [were] caught up at their highest point."

Several cowboys froze to death in Montana's Madison Valley, as did entire trainloads of cattle. Temperatures plummeted to -65 degrees at Fort Keogh, near Miles City—a U.S. record low for more than forty years. The *Perry* (Iowa) *Chief* sarcastically declared: "Last summer the mercury went up to 130 degrees above zero [at the outpost]…There is evidently no halfway work about the weather there."

The Blizzard of 1888's final toll was an estimated 235 people dead across the Northern Plains.

Her "The Grand" bordello, at the corner of State and Joliet streets in Helena, finally was razed during 1970s urban renewal.

# CHICAGO JOE

**Josephine Hensley, a poor Irish immigrant, became "the Queen of Helena's Red Light District."**

At age twenty-three, in 1867, she left Chicago's infamous tenderloin and headed for Helena. In a log cabin, she founded the mining camp's first house of ill repute. With orchestral music and a steady supply of new recruits from the Windy City, her business flourished. Customers christened this colorful madam "Chicago Joe."

Joe mortgaged everything, including "three dozen pair of underclothes," to acquire more property. She partnered with affluent businessmen and assembled a seedy empire in Helena.

Chicago Joe bankrolled the construction of the Coliseum, a vaudeville theater with curtained boxed seats where "painted ladies" offered "private entertainments."

CHICAGO JOE'S 1889 VALENTINE
MASQUERADE BALL
HAD JOURNALISTS JABBERING:

*"Orgies were the order of the evening... Frail coquettes in silken tights and [low-cut] bodices...glided to the...melodic music...forming a picture pleasing to behold."*

Joe became one of Helena's largest landowners. Her *New York Times* obituary noted the taxes she paid "on nearly $200,000 in property."

But the nationwide Panic of 1893 found Chicago Joe financially overextended. She lost virtually everything and died of pneumonia, nearly penniless, in 1899. Still, the local press remembered her as "a woman of extraordinary strength of character."

*Fire horses that were killed in the 1895 "awful calamity" in Butte.* Montana Historical Society Research Center Photograph Archives, Helena

# BUTTE RAIL YARD EXPLOSION OF 1895

**The press called it an "Awful Calamity—The Greatest Holocaust in the History of Butte or the West."**

On January 15, 1895, firemen approached a burning warehouse in the Montana Central Railway Yards. They didn't know that inside was a huge dynamite stockpile. The explosion "rocked Butte to its core."

The *New York Times* reported: "The shock shattered buildings...and rent limb from limb men within 300 yards...It wiped out of existence...the fire Department, killing men and horses and converting fire engines into heaps of twisted...metal."

A large, stunned crowd gathered. Then the second explosion hit—and the third. The Lincoln, Nebraska, *Evening News* noted: "The people in the vicinity were mown down as with a great scythe and the streets for half a block around looked like a great battlefield..."

**RENO'S *DAILY NEVADA STATE JOURNAL* DESCRIBED:**

*"Fragments of bodies...strewn in every direction...mangled and unrecognizable remains were scattered far and wide."*

Fifty-seven souls died in "the greatest explosion in the history of the West." The disaster killed bystanders and all but three fireman—including the chief and all the horses.

Describing the funerals that followed, an *Anaconda Standard* journalist wrote: "All day long the...bell tolled. Although the sun smiled from a clear sky, the bright sun seemed a mockery while every eye was dimmed with tears."

*Mary Fields, in a photographer's studio, did not seem as mean as her rifle would indicate.*

# STAGECOACH MARY FIELDS

**Though once a slave, Mary Fields answered to no man.**

Born on a Tennessee plantation in 1832, Fields was hell on wheels. Biographer Eunice Boeve wrote: "She was…about six feet tall and 200 pounds with…the strength and, sometimes the temperament[,] of a grizzly bear. But she also possessed the wit and warmth to charm even the coldest heart. She was unique. The kind of woman who gives rise to legends."

Montana cowboy and film star Gary Cooper knew Fields when he was a child.

### ACTOR GARY COOPER SAID FIELDS WAS:

*"One of the freest souls ever to draw a breath or a .38."*

Fields moved to Montana when her former master's daughter became headmistress at Saint Peter's Indian Boarding School. At the mission, she worked as a teamster, carpenter, and woodchopper, and one-woman security force, but following a shootout with a cowpuncher, church authorities fired her.

Historian Kelli Cardenas Walsh declared: "[Mary Fields] broke more noses than any other person in central Montana…[and] did not allow restrictions of race, gender, or age to define her."

At sixty-three, Fields became the first African American woman to deliver the U.S. mail. People called her "Stagecoach Mary." When snowdrifts stopped her horses, she strapped on snowshoes, shouldered the mail sack, and completed her fourteen-mile route.

Stagecoach Mary Fields died in 1914 at Cascade. Historian Darlene Clark Hine considered her "one of the most colorful characters in the history of the Great Plains."

*In 1885, J. Keppler portrayed Mark Twain's speaking style for the American magazine* Puck.

# MARK TWAIN TOURS MONTANA

**Mark Twain, America's favorite author, made a Montana speaking tour in 1895.** He was fifty-nine and deeply in debt from failed investments. Twain's only option for avoiding bankruptcy was, in his words, to "mount the platform…or starve."

Twain's stage performances were marvelous. Historian Rufus Coleman declared: "His tangled shock of once sandy hair…his ambling walk, his slow drawl, his sense of pause for the right word…and his deadpan look at the climatic moment—these were irresistible."

Twain made five Montana stops. He delighted Great Falls reporters by claiming that theirs was "one of the prettiest towns in the West…"

Hundreds packed Butte's Maguire's Opera House to hear what the *Butte Miner* called: "the droll genius whose quaint humor and native wit have sent refreshing waves of rippling laughter around the world." Twain filled the evening with tales of Calaveras County jumping frogs, Tom Sawyer, and Huckleberry Finn.

THE *ANACONDA STANDARD* PROCLAIMED:

*"Mark's All Right: He Can Keep an Audience in an Uproar Without an Effort."*

Twain's diary declared: "Beautiful audience. Compact, intellectual and dressed in perfect taste. It surprised me to find this London-Parisian-New York audience out in the mines."

Twain went on to visit Anaconda, Helena, and Missoula, before returning home safe and once again solvent. He never returned to Montana.

*So-called "Friend of the Indians," George Bird Grinnell*

# THE GRINNELL AGREEMENT OF 1895

**North-central Montana's Little Rocky Mountains were sacred to Fort Belknap Reservation's Gros Ventre and Assiniboine Indians.** By the 1890s, however, trespassing miners had found large gold deposits there.

Railroad magnate James J. Hill demanded a land sale. Fort Belknap's Indians resisted. Agent Joseph Kelley reported: "[T]he headmen of both tribes...unanimously agreed not to consider...diminishing...their present holdings under any circumstances...They claim that they are making strenuous efforts to become self-supporting, and...their posterity can work these mines to the best tribal advantage."

Hill vowed: "[I'll] do anything in [my] power to bring about the proposed cession of [Indian] lands..." He swore to "take the matter up personally with the Secretary of the Interior..."

In October of 1895, Hill got his wish—a treaty commission headed by noted naturalist George Bird Grinnell.

### DURING NEGOTIATIONS, GRINNELL DECLARED:

*"If you don't make an agreement with the government, you will just have to sell your cattle and then you will starve."*

Gros Ventre participant Sleeping Bear stated: "These Indians are all talking different, and I don't know what to do."

In the end, Grinnell—the so-called "Friend of the Indians," narrowly convinced an impoverished majority of Fort Belknap residents to sell for a mere $360,000 in annuities distributed over ten years.

Since the infamous Grinnell Agreement of 1895, non-natives have extracted more than $1 billion in gold from the Little Rocky Mountains.

*Named "buffalo soldiers" by Indians for their short-cut curly hair, members of the 25th Infantry Bicycle Corps prepare to pedal from western Montana to St. Louis.* MANSFIELD LIBRARY, UNIVERSITY OF MONTANA–MISSOULA

# FORT MISSOULA'S BICYCLE CORPS

**In 1897, General Nelson A. Miles proposed a new means of military transport: the bicycle.**

In 1897, Miles formed the 25th Infantry Bicycle Corps, stationed at Fort Missoula. In accordance with army regulations, Lieutenant James A. Moss, a white man, commanded the African-American unit.

Their mission: a 1900-mile, two-wheeled, self-propelled, cross-country expedition. Moss described his "buffalo soldiers" as "bubbling over with enthusiasm...about as fine a looking and well disciplined a lot as could be found anywhere..."

Pedaling state-of-the-art, seventy-pound bicycles, the 25th left Missoula for St. Louis, Missouri, on June 14, 1897. Despite steep hills and muddy roads, their bumpy trek took just thirty-four days.

### THE *SAINT LOUIS STAR* HAILED THE ADVENTURE AS:

*"The most marvelous cycling trip in the history of the wheel and the most rapid military march on record."*

Moss and his men had traveled twice as fast as a traditional cavalry could, at one-third the cost. Moss wrote: "The bicycle has a number of advantages over the horse...it needs no forage, it moves much faster over fair roads...it is noiseless and raises but little dust..."

But the bike's military success was no match for the newly invented gasoline engine. When the Spanish-American War broke out, the army disbanded its ground-breaking bicycle corps and sent the 25th Infantry to fight in Cuba and, later, the Philippines.

# ARCHITECT JOHN C. PAULSEN

**One of Montana's early architects—John C. Paulsen—was accused of faking his death to escape conviction in a major bribery scandal.**

The German-born Paulsen became Montana State Architect in 1895, overseeing state building projects including the Capitol designed by Bell & Kent.

Corrupt Capitol Commission members floated excessive bonds to build the statehouse, then pocketed millions. Fred Whiteside, a Kalispell legislator, exposed their fraud. He wrote: "[The swindle] was...done...by using cement, terra cotta and other cheap materials in place of the cut stone, bronze and copper specified."

Paulsen was Whiteside's primary informant. Historian Kirby Lambert wrote: "To convict...the commission, Paulsen would also have to indict himself for his involvement in similar schemes related to other state building projects."

In 1897—on the night before his grand jury testimony—Paulsen visited Whiteside.

**WHITESIDE RECALLED PAULSEN'S LAST NIGHT:**

*"[P]erspiration streamed from his face... He paced the floor,...saying 'God, they've got me...By God, I'll not [testify], but I know what I can do."*

The next morning Paulsen was dead. The *Herald* declared: "No Doubt that there was Crooked Work...Important Evidence Lost..."

Paulsen's wife arranged a closed-casket funeral the next day, raising further suspicion. The *Herald* reported that witnesses saw Paulsen in Great Falls and Denver. To quiet rumors, Paulsen's body was exhumed. His heart-attack death was confirmed, the insurance paid. Days later, Paulsen's wife left town, taking his coffin.

Without his testimony, Capitol Commission members were never indicted, but Governor Robert Smith disbanded the shady group. A new commission successfully completed Montana's statehouse in 1902.

*The Montana Capitol was designed by Bell and Kent, not by Paulsen. But, as State Architect overseeing all projects, he should have prevented the commission's graft.*

*The Paulsen-designed Jefferson County Courthouse in Boulder.*

*While kneading bread dough, Cameron took this self-portrait.* MONTANA HIS-
TORICAL SOCIETY RESEARCH CENTER PHOTOGRAPH ARCHIVES, HELENA

# EVELYN CAMERON

**Evelyn Cameron was Eastern Montana's Victorian feminist photographer.** Biographer Donna Lucey observed: "She seemed to... harvest the very energy of her surroundings and turn that power into a refined way of living..."

Cameron was born on a rambling English estate in 1868. Following her Montana honeymoon, Cameron and husband Ewen settled on a hard-scrabble ranch near Terry.

Cameron was nearly arrested for wearing what, at the time, was a shocking slit skirt to simplify horseback riding. Her pets included an antelope, hawks, and a pair of wolf cubs. She declared: "Manual labor...will really make a strong woman. I like to break colts, brand calves, cut down trees, ride and work in a garden."

Cameron's photography brought in extra income. She braved snake-infested terrain, lugging her camera and tripod to document prairie weddings, sheep shearings, desolate badlands, and all manner of wildlife.

### JOURNALIST MALCOLM JONES WROTE:

*"[Cameron] went after everything around her...Men, women, and children of all economic and ethnic backgrounds stand on an equal footing before her camera."*

Fifty years after her 1928 death, researchers unearthed Cameron's astounding legacy—thousands of dust-covered glass-plate negatives and original photographic prints, and 35 handwritten journals. Author Kurt Wilson called the discovery "one of the most detailed records...of life on the Great Plains."

*Little Bear, chief of the Cree in
Montana*

*The Chippewa chief, Stone Child, also was called
Rocky Boy.*

# ROCKY BOY INDIANS

**By the late 1880s, most Montana Indians lived on reservations.** But the Plains Cree still roamed, desperately seeking a home.

### CHIEF LITTLE BEAR DECLARED:

*"God was taking care of us...until the white man came...[N]ow our wives and... children [live] on dogs and the carcasses of frozen horses..."*

In 1888, Indian Affairs Commissioner John Atkins said: "I think [these refugees] should be given a chance to earn their bread, when that is all they ask."

Most Montanans were less sympathetic. The *River Press* editorialized: "the day has...passed when these lazy, dirty, lousy, breech-clothed, thieving savages can...nose around in the backyards..."

In 1896, "buffalo soldiers" from Fort Assinniboine raided and burned tent camps, and forced Little Bear's Cree into Canada. But they came back, scavenging dumps and slaughterhouses. Whites—fearing smallpox—drove them from Kalispell and Billings.

Then North Dakota Chippewas, close allies, arrived. Their Chief Rocky Boy was assertive and charismatic, and Little Bear deferred to Rocky Boy in "a joint effort to win a reservation for Indians...merging into a single tribe," according to historian Larry Burt.

In 1902 Rocky Boy convinced attorney J.W. James to write President Roosevelt. An investigation resulted. In 1916, President Wilson established the Rocky Boy Indian Reservation. Rocky Boy died a year later.

*James Willard Schultz, right, with his Blackfeet friend Many Tail Feathers.*

# JAMES WILLARD SCHULTZ

**"[He] did what many men only dreamed of—he lived with [and] fought beside Montana's fierce Blackfeet nation in its last glory days"**—that's writer David Peterson describing fur trader, explorer, anthropologist, and author James Willard Schultz.

In 1876, at seventeen years old, Schultz came to Montana from his native New York with a dream of hunting buffalo. Journalist Betsy Cohen has written that "[Schultz] was quickly swept into the ever-changing tide of …a wild and woolly frontier he would capture forever in numerous books and stories…"

Schultz learned the Blackfeet language, stole horses, and went on the warpath. He explored Glacier National Park, naming many landforms, including Going-to-the-Sun Mountain. When he married tribal member Fine Shield Woman, elders gave Schultz the name Apikuni, meaning "Far-off White Robe."

### BIOGRAPHER WARREN HANNA WROTE THAT SCHULTZ:

*"Began to see the world through the eyes of the Blackfeet."*

Schultz wrote thirty-seven books and scores of real-life adventure stories. His work, according to Professor Starr Jenkins, "show[s] us that a sympathetic heart and an eager mind can penetrate an alien culture and become a living and constructive part of it."

Environmental writer Don Snow said Schultz "[p]erhaps more than any other Montana writer…lived on the line between two worlds at the very moment when one century, one era, turned into another…He] still has the power today to…make that reader ache with a realization of what has been lost."

Schultz died in 1947 at the age of eighty-eight.

*Barbered and dressed up in Fort Worth, Texas, "Kid Curry" (standing at right) joined fellow Wild Bunch members for this 1900 studio portrait. To his right stands William "News" Carver, who liked seeing his name in newspapers; seated left to right are "the Sundance Kid" Harry Longabaugh, "the tall Texan" Ben Kilpatrick, and Robert Leroy Parker, "Butch Cassidy."*

# KID CURRY

**Harvey Logan, better known as Kid Curry, was "the Napoleon of Crime"—one of Montana's most notorious outlaws.**

William Pinkerton, founder of the famed Pinkerton Detective Agency, put it bluntly: "[Curry] has not one single redeeming feature…He is the only criminal I know of who doesn't have one single good point."

Dark and slightly bow-legged, with a prominent nose, Curry broke horses in Texas before working on his brother's ranch near north-central Montana's Little Rocky Mountains. In 1894 he killed miner "Pike" Landusky, then fled into his legendary life of crime. Based in Wyoming's Powder River Country, the Curry gang robbed banks, held up trains, and was involved in several shootouts with posses and civilians. By 1897, Curry was wanted dead or alive. The reward: $18,000.

TO HISTORIAN JAMES HORAN, KID CURRY WAS:

*"The most dangerous man in America's Wild West."*

In 1901, Curry joined forces with Butch Cassidy and the Sundance Kid, and gained a reputation as "the wildest of the Wild Bunch"—a group author that John Alwin calls: "one of the most awesome assemblages of outlaws the West had ever known." On July 3 that year, the gang hit the Great Northern express train between Malta and Wagner. Curry blew the safe and took $40,000. It was Montana's most famous train robbery.

Kid Curry is thought to have murdered at least nine law enforcement officers and at least two other people.

The specifics of Curry's death are unknown. Some say he shot himself in Colorado. Others say he made it to South America. But here in Montana, for decades, old timers swore they saw the Kid everywhere from Malta to Big Sandy.

*The Butte Miners' Union, Local #1, on parade in the early 20th century.*

# BUTTE MINERS UNION (PART 1)

**Butte—Montana's Mining City—became a union town on June 13, 1878.**

When mine owners at the Lexington and Alice slashed wages, 115 disgruntled miners organized. They formed the Butte Workingmen's Union, then sparked the first strike in Montana's history.

Shopkeepers, who were economically dependent on Butte's miners, supported the walkout. Hundreds joined the Union. By August, the mine owners restored wages. Historian Paul Frisch wrote: "[The strike] left a legacy of militancy and solidarity."

The renamed Butte Miners Union grew to 4,000 members. It became the first local of the militant Western Federation of Miners. The BMU demanded health benefits, burial expenses, and one of America's first eight-hour days.

Butte's *Daily Inter Mountain* praised the union as: "The most independent, most orderly, temperate and prosperous body of workingmen in the world."

Labor organizer Big Bill Haywood called it "the greatest single social force of the working class in…western…America."

The *Anaconda Standard* crowed: "From a barren treasury, [the BMU] has prospered until it is without a doubt the strongest union…in the country. It owns stock in the Amalgamated Copper company, it has a comfortable balance in the bank…and it…has loaned…in the neighborhood of a quarter of a million dollars to…miners in other parts of the West."

### HISTORIAN RICHARD LINGENFELTER, SAID THAT BY 1900 BUTTE WAS:

*"The strongest union town on earth."*

*During its heyday, downtown Anaconda was anchored by a grand hotel.*

# ANACONDA

**Anaconda was Montana's "smelter city."** Historian Michael P. Malone called it "one of the classic 'company towns' of the American West."

In 1883, copper king Marcus Daly assembled the raucous town from scratch. He bankrolled a mammoth copper-smelting complex that brought Butte and Anaconda to national prominence.

Corporate tentacles wrapped around every aspect of Anaconda life. Daly controlled the town's leading bank, newspaper, department store, and hotel. He donated land for churches, libraries, and parks. Historian Patrick Morris commented: "Buildings sprang up like mushrooms after a rain."

Journalist Si Stoddard stated that Daly hoped his fiefdom would be "the city of cities, a model for other municipalities."

In 1919, the Anaconda Company erected the 585-foot Anaconda Smelter smokestack. Large enough to swallow the Washington Monument, the towering landmark is still the world's tallest free-standing masonry structure.

### LONG-TIME RESIDENT BOB VINE RECALLED:

*"Everybody would get up in the morning and...look to see if there was smoke coming out of that stack... [I]f there was, God was in His Heaven, and all was right with the world...."*

But Anaconda's blue-collar existence screeched to a halt on "Black Monday," September 29, 1980. Faced with faltering global markets, the company's new owner, Atlantic Richfield, suddenly closed Anaconda's smelter. Today, the dormant stack reminds Montanans of the region's once dominant copper-smelting industry.

*Columbia Gardens offered fresh air, flowers, and green grass to Butte residents.* Montana Historical Society Research Center Photograph Archives, Helena

# COLUMBIA GARDENS

**Columbia Gardens—"the garden spot of the Rockies"—once sat three miles east of the gritty mining city of Butte.**

Historian Dave Walter wrote that "this combination of city park, athletic fields, banquet and dancing facility, and lake resort would have been remarkable in any setting. As a contrast to the greatest copper mining operation in the nation, it was amazing."

Butte resident Bob Kovacich recalled: "[A]ny person who visited would immediately fall in love with the place. It was better than Disneyland or any other amusement park in the entire country."

Copper King William Andrews Clark began developing his lush 68-acre paradise in 1899. Admission was free.

### CLARK BOASTED:

*"The Columbia Gardens is my monument. Of my many business enterprises it is the one that I love best, and it is practically the only one on which I lose money."*

Author Adolph Heilbronner observed: The Gardens' surroundings were "calculated to drive away the cares of men, to make them forget that Butte is such a terribly dusty, smoky, barren place."

But, during the 20th century, Butte's mines inched ever closer and—despite a deafening cry of opposition—the Anaconda Company closed Columbia Gardens to expand open-pit mining in 1973. Shortly thereafter, the park was gutted by fire and demolished.

Author Pat Kearney remembers: "The Columbia Gardens was like a William Shakespeare play. It was filled with beauty and grace, but closed with sorrow and tragedy."

*Mary MacLane, looking appropriately rebellious*

# MARY MacLANE

**Mary MacLane was "The Wild Woman of Butte."**

Born in 1881, MacLane was raised there. She called the city: "a pungent little place" that "devours…feminine youth with the jaws…of a monstrous insatiate demon."

In 1902, at age nineteen, MacLane published *The Story of Mary MacLane*. In it, she openly discussed her hunger for fame, her bisexual passions—even her desire to marry the Devil. MacLane confessed: "my head broke out in brains and I wrote my wail of adolescence…"

The mainstream press was horrified, but *The Story of Mary MacLane* quickly sold 100,000 copies.

### ANTHOLOGIST ELISABETH PRUITT WROTE:

*"She captured the fancy of millions…
was elevated to near-mythic status in her
own time…was gossiped about incessantly,
imitated constantly,
and condemned mercilessly."*

MacLane took her royalties to Greenwich Village. There she lived a decadent, Bohemian life as a journalist, gambler, and prize-fight reporter. She wrote and starred in her own silent movie—*Men Who Have Made Love to Me*—then faded into obscurity.

Asked what would happen if she ever reached age twenty-five, a young MacLean boasted: "I don't care. But I shall not be forgotten…I am one of the great ones of earth."

When, at 48, MacLane died penniless, a Jazz Age magazine—*The Chicagoan*—remembered her as "the first of the self-expressionists…the first of the flappers."

# THE GREAT SHUTDOWN

**Butte's "handsome, industrial desperado" was the predatory mining engineer, Fritz Augustus Heinze.** Historian Joseph Kinsey Howard called him "The most adept pirate in the history of American capitalist privateering…"

At age twenty, with a Columbia University degree and a huge inheritance, Heinze descended upon Montana. He quickly bought up profitable mining properties and became Butte's youngest "copper king." Heinze bribed judges to skew legal interpretations and made millions more acquiring rich mineral veins.

In 1903, Heinze-controlled courts ruled against the mighty Amalgamated Copper Company—a subsidiary of Standard Oil. Amalgamated countered with "the Great Shutdown."

The corporate giant abruptly closed its doors. Twenty thousand miners, smeltermen, lumbermen, and railroad workers—four-fifths of Montana's wage earners—were jobless. The *Flathead Herald Journal* wrote: "We believe that a deep, dark, damnable game is being played."

## FROM THE BALCONY OF BUTTE'S COURTHOUSE, HEINZE CAUTIONED 10,000 LAID-OFF MINERS:

*"If they crush me today they will crush you tomorrow… They will cut your wages… They will force you to dwell in Standard Oil houses while you live, and they will bury you in Standard Oil coffins when you die."*

But Governor Joseph Toole wanted to placate "The Company." A special legislative session passed a "fair trials" bill enabling Amalgamated to disqualify Heinze's judges.

Now on the ropes, Heinze soon sold out, returning to New York. He died several years later. *The Philadelphia Inquirer* wrote: "Heinze's fight may have been worthwhile…but his early death in comparative poverty illustrates how devious are the ways of the speculator and how dangerous is the game."

*F. Augustus Heinze*

*The Fort Shaw championship basketball team*

# FORT SHAW WORLD CHAMPIONS

**One of the finest girls' basketball teams ever came from Montana—the Fort Shaw Indian School, west of Great Falls.** They were virtually undefeated between 1902 and 1906.

Playing boys' rules, the ten-girl team from seven tribes battled all comers. They traveled the state, dazzling sellout crowds and crushing opponents in Butte, Helena, and Missoula. In Bozeman, they defeated the state agricultural college Farmerettes *twice*, holding them scoreless in one game.

The *Anaconda Standard* reported: their "particularly entertaining" style had "much to do with making the game so popular in Montana."

On train trips outside the Treasure State, the Fort Shaw team took on local challengers in exhibition contests. Then they donned ceremonial buckskin dresses and presented cultural programs for extra travel money.

At the 1904 St. Louis World's Fair, the team stole the show. Playing for nearly three million spectators in multiple games, they defeated everyone—including men's teams. They came back to Montana with a silver trophy proclaiming them "The World Champions of Girls Basketball."

Prejudiced newspapers everywhere called them "dusky belles" and "dark complexioned maidens," but they always praised the team's stamina, skill, and discipline.

IN THEIR BOOK *FULL COURT QUEST*, LINDA PEAVY AND URSULA SMITH WROTE:

*The girls from Fort Shaw "overcame barriers of gender, race, and class to emerge as champions...shattering stereotypes concerning the athletic, academic, and artistic capabilities of Native American girls and women."*

*Ella Knowles*

*Ella Knowles married Montana State Attorney Henri Haskell after he won that office in 1892 by defeating her; they divorced ten years later.*

# ELLA KNOWLES

**Ella Knowles was Montana's ground-breaking feminist attorney.**
Historian Dave Walter called her "one of [Montana's] most accomplished
progressive women."

Knowles became the first woman to practice law in the Treasure State.
Upon her unprecedented admission to the Montana bar, esteemed Judge
Cornelius Hedges proclaimed: "She beat all that I have ever examined."

Knowles was the first woman in the nation to run for office as a state Attorney General. Newspapers applauded the Populist Party candidate for
debunking the old myth of women's "intellectual and moral inferiority,"
calling her a "silver tongued orator."

Less progressive critics complained Knowles spoke in "a monotonous
tone of voice…with a New England accent, which rendered Montana as
'Maun-ta-na.'" Another detractor suggested that some "good man" ought
to "protect [Knowles] from the shocks of political life by marrying her."

Knowles narrowly lost her election, but gained a reputation as a "remark-
ably plucky fight[er]." While serving as Montana Women Suffrage Association president, she led 2500 supporters to Helena, arguing: "If it was
unjust for our fathers to be taxed by Great Britain without representation,
it is unjust to tax women today without representation."

## IN 1907, *THE ANACONDA STANDARD* DECLARED:

*"There is not a practicing attorney in the
courts of Montana who is regarded with
greater respect…"*

Knowles died in Butte in 1911. The University of Montana named
Knowles Hall in her honor.

*The first Hauser Dam, made of steel, was believed to show the material of the future. It was one of a handful of such experiments, and survived only a year.* MONTANA HISTORICAL SOCIETY RESEARCH CENTER PHOTOGRAPH ARCHIVES, HELENA

# HAUSER DAM

**Hauser Dam is fifteen miles downstream on the Missouri River from Helena.** Designing engineers called it "one of the greatest projects of the age" until April 1908, when disaster struck.

For weeks, massive flooding had pounded western Montana. Then the year-old structure's steel plates buckled. Silt-laden water gushed out.

## A WORKER YELLED:

## *"Flee for your lives; the dam is breaking!"*

Minutes later, a 300-foot section of the dam burst. The gaping hole drained all twenty square miles of Hauser Lake. That deluge of water tore down the Missouri River.

The *Wall Street Journal* reported: "The town of Craig, with a population of 400[,] has probably been wiped out…The town of Cascade…is under water and in danger of being swept away. An avalanche of water threatens the city of Great Falls …"

The *New York Times* wrote: "The surface of the flood is black with ranch houses, livestock, and haystacks."

In Great Falls, detached houses and farm buildings smashed into the Great Northern Railroad Bridge. Panicked townsfolk dynamited the Black Eagle Dam to prevent an even greater disaster.

Floodwaters filled with toxic waste from the Boston & Montana smelter turned Fort Benton into "a Montana Venice." Cattleman William Witt told company officials "[M]y ranch looks as if you selected it for the dumping grounds of the silt and slag of your smelter…" Attorneys concluded the river, not the dam owner, was responsible.

Hauser Dam's failure caused $3 million in damages. Engineers finally rebuilt the structure in 1911.

*Missoula's Higgins Avenue bridge collapsed into the Clark Fork River during the 1908 flood.*

# MISSOULA'S FLOOD OF 1908

**May and June 1908 brought a month of hard rain to western Montana—the worst downpour in Treasure State history.**
Headlines dubbed it "the inundation of Montana." The *New York Tribune* related: "Every little trout stream…is a raging torrent[,]…[rivers] are twice their usual width and overflowing the lowlands…"

A burst power plant dam plunged Butte into darkness. Poisonous mine waste flooded Deer Lodge Valley farmland.

In Missoula, streetcars, telegraphs, and electric lights failed. Three feet of water covered the streets. Neighborhoods, one resident said, "looked like Lake Michigan."

## AN EYEWITNESS SAID:

*"The houses came down the stream looking just as they did when they stood upon solid ground until they struck the steel Northern Pacific bridge… Then they crumpled like houses of cards and disappeared into the flood."*

The *Daily Missoulian* reported: "Great crowds stood…watching the sheds, pieces of furniture, and quantities of driftwood that were carried down stream and speculating on the possibility of a break in the Clark dam at Bonner." Late one night, the center of Missoula's Higgins Avenue Bridge washed out as the Great Flood of 1908 crested.

All told, thirty railroad bridges were destroyed. Hundreds of passengers were stranded for weeks. The *Wenatchee Daily World* called it "the largest single loss…by a natural catastrophe…ever suffered by the Northern Pacific Railroad." Engineers and mechanics took nine weeks to complete the repairs.

*Elizabeth Gurley Flynn as a youthful orator*

# ELIZABETH GURLEY FLYNN AND MISSOULA'S FREE SPEECH FIGHT

The *Butte Miner* called labor organizer Elizabeth Gurley Flynn the "arch disturber…a woman of considerable power… and…unquestioned courage…"

Born in 1890, Elizabeth Gurley Flynn joined the radical union the Industrial Workers of the World as a teenager. At nineteen, she came to Missoula to protest a ban on street speech. She and her fellow IWW "wobblies" stood on soapboxes reading the U.S. Constitution and the Declaration of Independence, openly defying the law. Flynn warned: "The crowds seem to be in full accord…woe betide the fellow that dares object!"

Firemen drenched the protesters. Cops locked Flynn and dozens of others in a filthy, crowded jail. A local preacher called the treatment "too good for a lot of damned anarchists."

The IWW called on "every free born 'American'…who hates…tyrannical oppression…to go to Missoula… [and] give 'em hell!" Hundreds packed the jails. It was "the West's first full-fledged free-speech fight."

### FLYNN RECALLED:

*"At first the police were very full of fight… But when the [entire] force had to get out night after night…they began to lose interest in the fun."*

The City Council eventually dropped all charges. *The Industrial Worker* newspaper proclaimed: "An I.W.W. man can now go to Missoula…and talk on any street in town."

Flynn later helped found the American Civil Liberties Union. She died on a visit to the Soviet Union in 1964.

*Strong muscles and hand tools were the only weapons for fighting the Big Burn.*

# THE BIG BURN OF 1910

**The largest forest fire in American history was the Big Burn of 1910.** In just two days, three million acres burned in Washington, Idaho, and Montana.

The blaze incinerated town after town. Frantic telegrams pled for help. Rescue trains raced across burning trestles to save hundreds of townspeople. Meanwhile, ten thousand men—including Indians and even skid-row bums brought from Spokane—frantically battled the Big Burn.

### JOURNALIST JIM PETERSON DESCRIBED THE CHAOS:

*"In a matter of hours, fires became firestorms, and trees by the millions became exploding candles. Millions more, sucked from the ground, roots and all, became flying blowtorches... [W]ind-powered fireballs...rolled from ridgetop to ridgetop at seventy miles an hour...Entire mountainsides ignited in an instant. It was like nothing anyone had ever seen before."*

Early snows finally doused the fire. Firefighter Joe Halm witnessed the aftermath: "The green standing forest of yesterday was gone; in its place, a charred and smoking mass of melancholy wreckage."

The Big Burn of 1910 torched enough timber to fill a freight train 2,400 miles long. Eighty-six people died. As forester William Greeley put it: "Congress…now realized that fire protection was the number one job of the Forest Service."

*Charles M. Bair, in from the fields*

**"Charlie" Bair was "The Great Flockmaster of Montana" and "King of the Western Wool Growers."** Biographer Lee Rostad observed: "[Bair] was always busy with both...hands and his head."

Born in 1857, Bair left his Ohio home, worked on Montana's Northern Pacific Railroad, saved up, and bought ranches. In 1898, he scrambled north in the Klondike gold rush. A business partner remarked: "Charlie is just the type for a trip to Alaska ...and is probably selling snowballs to the Eskimos."

Bair did make a fortune: selling hot-air machines that thawed frozen mining ground. He later called on a boyhood friend, President William McKinley, and pulled out a jaw-dropping handful of gold nuggets. McKinley declared: "Charlie, you handle nuggets the way we handled shell corn down in Ohio!"

Back in Montana, Bair leased Crow Reservation lands and ran about 300,000 head of sheep. Bair's 1910 shearing filled forty-seven railroad cars.

### TRAIN BANNERS BOASTED:

*"The largest wool clip grown by one individual on the North American Continent."*

The flamboyant Bair raced cars and hobnobbed with Teddy Roosevelt, Tom Mix, and Charlie Russell. He retired near Martinsdale, building a "prairie palace," its rooms brimming with Louis XV furnishings and other European antiques his daughters added.

Charlie Bair died in 1945 and was inducted into the National Cowboy Hall of Fame. His home is now open to the public as the Bair Family Museum.

Gregson Hot Springs Hotel, Natatorium 200x64,
Boyce-Butte, 17 Miles from Butte, Mont.

*Gregson Hot Springs offered a sedate setting for the 1912 riot.*

# THE GREGSON PICNIC OF 1912

**Fairmont, eleven miles west of Butte, was originally named Gregson Hot Springs.** The *Anaconda Leader* called it: "the resort for workers of Butte City, as well as for the thousands of toiling miners, a place of rest and relaxation."

This was hardly the case, however, during the August 1912 Butte Miners Union Picnic for its six thousand members and their families. The same day the Anaconda Mill and Smelterman's Union also held their summer outing at the resort. Fourteen thousand of their people crowded Gregson's shaded groves for a day of contests, feasting, and heavy drinking.

Someone suggested a friendly tug-of-war between Butte's Irish miners and Anaconda's Serbian smeltermen. The strongest and heaviest men grabbed the rope. "Whiskey and beer flowed freely, intensifying the excitability and lowering the boiling points of participants and spectators alike," wrote author Patrick Morris.

The Butte team lost. Someone cried foul. Arguments led to traded punches, then chaos: Everyone in both unions dove into the drunken slugfest. Shots were fired. The crowds panicked and ran.

### THE BUTTE *DAILY MINER* REPORTED:

*"The afternoon sun was hidden from sight by...clouds of flying bottles."*

Special trains hauled the wounded back to hospitals in Butte and Anaconda that night. Two men died. At the inquest, the judge could not figure out what happened, so no one was prosecuted.

*Belle Fligelman (later Mrs. Norman Winestine) when she worked in New York City as a young college graduate.*

# BELLE WINESTINE

**Historian Jeanne Abrams wrote of Belle Winestine "[She was] feisty...one of a number a western Jewish female pioneers... who helped secure...suffrage...for women throughout the United States."**

Winestine was born in Helena in 1891. She grew into a five-foot-tall feminist dynamo, graduated from the University of Wisconsin, then became the *Helena Independent's* first female reporter, specializing in women's issues.

Winestine gained fame in Helena by shouting fiery feminism from soapboxes. Supporters described her as "a plucky little generalissimo."

### WINESTINE RECALLED:

*"No one in Montana...had ever heard of a respectable young woman making a public street corner speech. Yet we knew we would have to adopt all the normal political techniques if we were going to win the vote...My mother was horrified..."*

Montana women won the right to vote in 1914—six years before women achieved suffrage nationally—*then* elected Jeanette Rankin as America's first female member of Congress. Winestine became her administrative assistant. This, according to the *Jewish Woman's Archive:* "solidified what became her lifelong commitment to reform."

From World War I to Vietnam, Winestine fought for women's rights, children's issues, and peace. She died in 1985 at age ninety-four. In 1999, the *Missoulian* named Winestine one of the 100 most influential Montanans of the twentieth century.

*Butte Miners Union Hall after the explosions.* MONTANA HISTORICAL SOCIETY RESEARCH CENTER PHOTOGRAPH ARCHIVES, HELENA

# BUTTE MINERS UNION (PART 2)

**The Butte Miners Union was once known as "the Gibraltar of Unionism."** But in 1914, the publication *Mining and Engineering World* charged: "[Union leaders] have grown fat and prosperous while… thousands of Butte miners…have been living in squalor, and maintaining families at near starvation points."

Labor frustration exploded in what *The International Socialist Review* called: "a spontaneous uprising of the masses." Hundreds rioted while angry copper miners sacked the Miners Union Hall. From the building's second story, Mayor Frank Curran pleaded with the crowd. Their response: "Go to hell!" Then someone pushed the mayor out the window.

Chaos followed. Gun-toting miners combed the streets searching for the Union's "copper collared" leaders. Police officers closed saloons and ordered hardware stores to hide ammunition.

A week later, a mob of thousands again stormed the Union Hall. Shots rang out. Two men were killed. Union leaders scrambled to safety as twenty-six dynamite blasts reduced the headquarters to rubble.

### A CONNECTICUT NEWSPAPER REPORTED:

*"Hundreds of persons were struck by flying glass which rattled down upon the heads of people packed on the sidewalk every time a blast was set off."*

Governor Samuel Stewart declared martial law—troops patrolled the streets. The dominant Anaconda Company announced that it would no longer recognize any union in Butte.

Historians Michael Malone and Richard Roeder concluded: "The company had its way, and the mining labor movement in Butte lay broken and helpless."

*Granite Mountain Mine in full production*

*Commemorating the 168 victims of the Granite Mountain fire, an interpretive viewing area now looks down on the site.*

# THE GRANITE MOUNTAIN FIRE OF 1917

**On a June night in 1917, death came to Butte—home of the "Richest Hill on Earth."**

North Butte Mining Company Assistant Foreman Ernest Sullau accidentally ignited a fire 2400 feet within the Granite Mountain Mine. Flames roared up the shaft and into the night sky. Author Michael Punke wrote: "[Smoke] poured in a torrent, deluging the valley below and spreading out over the...hill like a giant shroud."

Fire and deadly carbon monoxide gas fanned through the stopes and shafts to connecting mines. Rescuers faced a pitch-black maze with hundreds of miles of underground passageways.

Deep underground, Granite Mountain shift boss James Moore died just before the rescue crew reached him. His last thoughts were recorded in a note to his wife: "Dear Pet...I tried to get all the men out, but the smoke was too strong...[I]f anything happens to me...know your Jim died like a man, and his last thoughts were of his wife that I have loved better than anybody on earth..."

Of the 410 miners working that night, 168 died. It was the deadliest disaster in metal mining history.

## THE BUTTE *DAILY POST* REPORTED:

*"Desolated homes, stricken townsmen, the bitter sacrifice of robust manhood, the unavailing tears, the shattering of hopes and the rude sundering of tender ties— these things fill the mind of this community."*

*Labor union martyr Frank Little*

# FRANK LITTLE

**Frank Little was a crippled, half-Cherokee labor agitator.** He came to Butte in 1917 to persuade striking miners to join the radical Industrial Workers of the World.

Little condemned U.S. involvement in World War I and urged workers to destroy the copper trust, even though copper was a crucial wartime commodity. He scorned American troops as "Uncle Sam's scabs in uniform."

### ADDRESSING THOUSANDS, LITTLE DECLARED:

*"Either we're for their capitalist slaughter fest or against it. I'm ready to face a firing squad rather than compromise."*

Little's fiery speeches enraged Montana's ultra-patriots and the powerful Anaconda Copper Mining Company. *The Butte Miner*, a company-owned newspaper, reported: "Frank Little [has]…practically threatened the United States government with revolution…[T]he speaker worked himself into a maniacal fury as he denounced the capitalist of every class and nationality…"

The paper demanded that authorities crack down on "incendiary agitators…spreading the doctrine of hatred." But in true Montana fashion, vigilantes acted first.

At 3:00 A.M. on August 1, 1917, six masked men broke into Little's room. Throwing his crutches aside, they beat him, tied him to the back of a car, and dragged him out of town. There, they lynched him from a north-side railroad trestle. A note, "First and last warning," was pinned to Little's chest.

Frank Little's murderers escaped justice. His weathered epitaph in Butte's Mountain View Cemetery reads simply: "Slain by Capitalist Interests for Organizing and Inspiring His Fellow Men."

*L.A. Huffman named this homesteader photograph "The Honyocker," appropriating an insult thrown at farmers by cattlemen.*

# HOMESTEAD BOOM

**The land is "fast being settled up with farmers, many of whom came to Montana as a better class of miners and, after quitting their original pursuits, secure 160 acres"**—that's how the *Montana Post* described the territory just two years after Abraham Lincoln signed the Homestead Act of 1862.

Montana was the most heavily homesteaded state in the union. Roughly half of the homesteaders had no farming experience. All were attracted by the government's offer of free land.

## AS ONE SODBUSTER PUT IT:

*"I was raised in Chicago without so much as a backyard to play in. When I heard that you could get 320 acres just by living on it, I felt that I had been offered a kingdom."*

Railroads enticed German and Scandinavian immigrants to eastern Montana with slogans like: "Wake up! Free land will soon be as scarce as hair on an egg" and "Montana is a gentle and generous mistress!"

For a time, those ads seemed true. Wheat prices skyrocketed. Rain fell. In 1915, the Montana Department of Agriculture noted: "Thousands of energetic farmers are here now, and they…are on the road to prosperity. So great an empire is this commonwealth that there is yet room for many thousands more…"

The early 20th century homestead boom more than tripled Montana's population to nearly 800,000, adding twenty-eight new counties and dozens of new boomtowns. But a bust would soon follow.

*Incorporated in 1909, the First State Bank of Chester built this downtown structure the following year, but the business failed in 1929. Originally, an oak turret rose from above the door to above the roofline. Chester High School Class of 1997 successfully nominated the building to the National Register of Historic Places, protecting its exterior from undue modernization.*

# HOMESTEAD BUST

**"Honyocker, scissorbill, nester...swarming into a hostile land; duped when he started, robbed when he arrived"**—that's author Joseph Kinsey Howard's description of the Montana homesteader.

They cobbled together makeshift shacks from grassy slabs of topsoil: they faced the blistering heat and subzero cold of Montana's sometimes-inhospitable plains. Homesteader Sue Howells recalled: "I have stood in the doorway of our shack, with my heart full of...loneliness, and listened to the wind. It is an incessant, screeching, whining and screaming wind and it seems to be heard nowhere except in Montana on the homestead."

After World War I, disaster struck. The *Havre Plaindealer* called the catastrophe "the worst in the history of the state." Historian Don Spritzer wrote: "Plagued by blowing dust, low crop prices, and hordes of insects, once optimistic settlers left in droves."

Between 1919 and 1925, eleven thousand farms were vacated.

### A POETIC SIGN ON ONE DEPARTING VEHICLE READ:

*"Twenty miles from water, forty miles from wood. We're leaving old Montana, and we're leaving for good!"*

Montana was the only state that lost population during the "roaring" 1920s, and the Great Depression was still to come.

As historian Dave Walter noted: "In Montana's litany of 'boom and bust cycles' the homestead era reigns supreme because it involved so many people and so much land."

*A ticket clerk for the Northern Pacific Rail Road in Missoula, A.B. Kimball, is dressed for a day at work during the 1918 flu pandemic.* MONTANA HISTORICAL SOCIETY RESEARCH CENTER PHOTOGRAPH ARCHIVES, HELENA

# THE INFLUENZA EPIDEMIC OF 1918

**The worst natural catastrophe of the 20th century was the Spanish influenza pandemic of 1918.** Forty million people died worldwide, including 675,000 in the United States.

Historian Pierce Mullen wrote: "In Montana, influenza's swath was broad, swift, and devastating." The state ranked fourth nationally in per capita deaths.

By mid-October 1918, Montana Chancellor of Education Edward C. Elliot acknowledged: "the influenza was spreading around the country like a medieval plague."

Health officials banned most public gatherings. Churches, schools, libraries, saloons, and movie houses were closed. Those infected were quarantined. Public buildings—including Bozeman's Gallatin County High School—became makeshift hospitals.

### THE *GREAT FALLS TRIBUNE* NOTED THAT IN BUTTE:

*"Undertakers no longer garage their 'dead wagons,' but leave them in the street as calls are so frequent..."*

In mid-November, World War I ended. The *Bozeman Chronicle* reported: "The entire county went wild over the signing of the armistice and forgot all about precautions and the epidemic." Flu cases skyrocketed.

By spring 1919, the outbreak was finally diminishing. Bans on public gatherings were lifted.

One-third of Montana's population had contracted the disease. About 5,000 Montanans—one percent of the state's population—had died from the virus.

*On a picnic outing, Nancy Russell sits at far right, next to her artist husband. The other couple is unidentified.*

# NANCY COOPER RUSSELL

**Nancy Cooper Russell was the driving force behind Montana's great cowboy artist—Charlie Russell.** Russell called her "the best booster and pardner a man ever had."

The couple married in 1896 and settled in Great Falls. Though she lacked education and was fourteen years younger than her spouse, Nancy helped turn a charismatic ranch hand, who sketched and sculpted in his spare time, into "the highest paid living artist of his time."

Western art critic Ginger K. Renner said: "It is difficult to overemphasize Nancy Cooper Russell's importance…[H]ad Charlie and Nancy not met…it is doubtful that Russell would have created the prodigious body of artwork…that is truly one of our most cherished national treasures."

Shortly after their marriage, Nancy started managing Russell's new career. In 1903, she scheduled a New York City trip to promote her husband's talent. Afterwards, the couple returned annually to rub elbows with artists, critics and patrons. Russell's popularity soared.

Museum Curator Pam Hendrickson said: "It was [Nancy's] drive and ambition that developed his reputation…She got exhibitions all over the country and internationally. She recognized his talent…and together they made a good team."

### IN 1919, CHARLIE RUSSELL TOLD A REPORTER:

*"My wife has been an inspiration to me… Without her I would probably have never attempted to soar or reach any height, further than to make a few pictures for my friends and old acquaintances…I still love and long for the old west, but I would sacrifice it all for Mrs. Russell."*

*For a small boy, the Neversweat on a peaceful, busy day was an intriguing sight.*

# THE ANACONDA ROAD MASSACRE

**Butte's Anaconda Road is the primary artery approaching the mines of "the richest hill on earth," and the site of deadly labor violence in 1920.**

The radical Industrial Workers of the World (IWW) had demanded higher wages and the release of "political prisoners." Angry workers blocked the gates of the Neversweat mine and confronted scabs trying to cross picket lines. The *New York Times* headlines warned: "Strikers are Massing and More Disorder is Feared…"

Butte Sheriff John O'Rourke—a pawn of the nearly omnipotent Anaconda Company—declared: "The present situation is not a labor strike, it is revolution." He deputized gun-toting mine guards and ordered protesters to disperse. Then a shot rang out. The *San Francisco Chronicle* reported: "in a second a hundred…guns were flashing."

Bullets cut through the panicked crowd as they ran down the hill. Striker Sam Embree recalled, "[b]ullets were whizzing around me …I saw several of my companions fall…" Sixteen picketers were shot in the back as they scrambled for cover. Tom Manning—an Irish miner—was killed. The incident became known as the "Anaconda Road Massacre." Sheriff O'Rourke and his deputies denied responsibility.

### THE *BUTTE BULLETIN* SARCASTICALLY ASKED:

*"Did the sixteen miners shoot themselves?"*

The outraged IWW called on Butte's workers to "lay down their tools and stop the wheels of industry." But federal troops imposed martial law and the strike was called off, with no gains for the workers.

No one was ever charged with the murder of Tom Manning.

# PLENTY COUPS

**Describing Plenty Coups, the diplomatic Crow leader, historian Norman Wiltsey declared: "Of all the great American Indian chiefs of the era of white encroachment, only one achieved...a fair and lasting peace with the white men and retention of the homeland of his people in perpetuity."**

Plenty Coups was born in 1848 near present Billings. At age nine, he climbed the Crazy Mountains. There he had a powerful, prophetic dream. He foresaw the buffalo's disappearance and the survival of the Crow Nation against insurmountable odds.

### PLENTY COUPS RECALLED HIS DREAM:

*"I saw the Four Winds gathering to strike [a] forest...[I] saw the beautiful trees twist like blades of grass and fall in tangled piles...Only one tree, tall and straight, was left standing..."*

Tribal elders interpreted the vision. The Crow people must adapt to the white society. The Crow forged alliances with whites to fight their traditional enemies, the Sioux and Cheyenne. Plenty Coups explained: "Our decision was reached, not because we loved the white man...but because we plainly saw that this course was the only one which might save our beautiful country..."

Other tribes were stripped of their territory and traditions. Plenty Coups accommodated, and preserved Crow lands and culture. He sought better schools, stating: "Education is your greatest weapon. With education you are the white man's equal, without education you are his victim..." His vision helped the Crow Nation transition from "buffalo days" to reservation life.

Plenty Coups died in 1932, still fighting for his people. The Crow headmen voted unanimously against choosing another chief. They declared: "No living man can fill Plenty Coups' place…therefore it is fitting that none be chosen."

*Two old campaigners met at the 1921 dedication of the Tomb of the Unknown Soldier in Washington, D.C.: Chief Plenty Coups at right, with Ferdinand Foch, commander of the French and Allied armies during World War I.*

*If anyone even complained about the U.S. government, Senator Meyers wanted to charge them with treason, a capital crime.*

# SENATOR HENRY MYERS

**The grandfather of U.S. anti-communist crusades was two-term (1911-1923) Democratic Senator Henry Myers of Montana.** During World War I, Myers was swept up in "the emotional wartime burst of patriotic fervor [that] engulfed Montana [and made] 'loyalty' a high priority," wrote historian Kurt Wetzel.

Myers saw labor unions as seedbeds of socialism, "the greatest menace facing this country today." After Russia's revolution, Myers predicted that, unless Congress suppressed unions, this "nation will see a Soviet government...within two years..."

## MYERS DECLARED:

*"We whipped the redskins to obtain possession of this country. We whipped the Red Coats to achieve its independence, and we must not let the red-hearted and red-handed overthrow it. 'Down the reds'... should now be our motto."*

Unions, Socialists, suffragists, radicals, Reds—Myers hated them all. In 1920, he condemned his own party's congressional nominees as "socialists and those preaching revolution." He switched parties, advocating voting Republican.

Myers also attacked motion pictures. He said Hollywood was a place where "debauchery, drunkenness, ribaldry, dissipation and free love seem to be conspicuous" and movies gave youth ideas "of fast life, shady ways, laxity of living, [and] loose morals." Myers unsuccessfully advocated government film censorship.

Disgusted, Myers retired from the Senate in 1923. He later served two years on Montana's Supreme Court, and died in 1943.

*The nefarious Young affects a genteel look for the camera.* MONTANA HISTORICAL SOCIETY RESEARCH CENTER PHOTOGRAPH ARCHIVES, HELENA

# HAVRE'S "SHORTY" YOUNG

**C.W. "Shorty" Young—a fast-talking, pint-sized reprobate—
was Havre's "king of vice."** He quickly formed an underworld empire.

From its dusty start in 1887, Havre was, as the *Chicago Mail-Tribune*
called it, "one wicked little town." Historian Don Spritzer declared: "A
volatile combination of railroaders, cowboys,...gamblers, prostitutes, and
soldiers..." made Havre "one of the roughest towns west of the Mississippi."

## IN 1916 THE LAW AND ORDER LEAGUE CONCLUDED:

*"Of all the communities visited, a
little city called Havre, Montana is
comparatively the worst...It is the sum
total of all that is vicious and depraved
parading openly without restraint..."*

Do-gooders made Prohibition the law of the land in 1920. Young smelled
a golden opportunity. His syndicate, "The Havre Bunch," illegally import-
ed booze from neighboring Canada. Their stated purpose: "To promote
cordial business relations between Montana and the Canadian Provinces."

Young's business boomed. Beneath Havre's streets an elaborate network
of secret passages, subterranean speakeasies, brothels, and opium dens
thrived throughout the "Roaring Twenties."

Federal agents finally stopped the Bunch in 1929. Fifty-two Havre businesses closed because of the crackdown.

A heart attack killed "Shorty" Young in 1944. The sizable endowment he
left financed various service organizations in Havre for decades.

*Carter County Attorney Ralph Nelstead, and county sheriff George Boggs, destroy a still during 1919.* Montana Historical Society Research Center Photograph Archives, Helena

# PROHIBITION FAILS IN MONTANA

**The Missoulian called it "the wake of John Barleycorn."** The *Helena Daily Independent* described "the quietest welcome a new year has received since Last Chance Gulch was first dug…" The year was 1919—the start of the United States' ill-advised Prohibition era.

Newspapers at first reported "the sale of intoxicants stopped absolutely." But shortly, historians Mike Malone and Richard Roeder observed, "prohibition failed all across the country, and nowhere more spectacularly than in Montana."

By 1921, federal authorities claimed that Butte led the nation in per capita consumption of illicit liquor. Treasure State rum-runners built the infamous Bootlegger Trail to Canada. Booze flowed into Montana from the north. Liquor revenues there increased fourfold. One Hi-Line Prohibition official complained: "No local assistance can be secured [in Montana] by federal officers in fighting the liquor traffic."

Many didn't consider violating Prohibition a serious crime. Great Falls resident Jeanette Bowen recalled: "It was no disgrace after Prohibition [began] if you bootlegged."

## THE *GREAT FALLS TRIBUNE* REPORTED:

*"The way in which boys and girls in their teens have become addicts of the 'hip flask' shocks the federal authorities."*

In 1926 Montana became the first state in the nation to repeal its own enforcement of Prohibition. Federal agents were on their own.

When "the great experiment" of Prohibition finally ended nationwide in 1933, most Montanans celebrated…with a stiff drink.

*A horseback contingent in the Bozeman Roundup parade*

# BOZEMAN ROUNDUP

**In the carefree summer after World War I, Montana promoters created a spectacular, three-day western show.** Its slogan was "She's Wild," an event to "surpass any like entertainment ever pulled off in the country." The Bozeman Roundup completely transformed the Gallatin Valley each year between 1919 and 1926.

Headlines proclaimed: "Ten Thousand Visitors in City—the Greatest Throng Ever Here." Automobiles clogged highways. Visitors packed hotels and private homes. Canvas tents completely covered local parks: as one camper put it: "a mosquito couldn't light comfortably without hitting one."

Della Doyle remembered: "It was really big…you just can't imagine the havoc…People…would just do everything in the world to prepare weeks ahead…"

America's best cowboys and cowgirls came to ride "notorious and unmanageable horses and bulls" hoping for a piece of the Roundup's impressive $6,000 purse. Overflowing crowds thrilled to stagecoach races, bulldogging from automobiles, Native American pow wows, and something called "drunken riding."

### ONE REPORTER GUSHED:

*"Oh boy! Oh boy! …Where do we go from here? You can go and watch 'em ride, or buck, or bet, or dance, or any old thing, if you follow the crowd in Bozeman during… this wild, wild roundup."*

Visitor J.L. Hart agreed that the event was "worth a trip across the continent…I never saw a better show in my life…"

# TIME

## The Weekly News-Magazine

WALSH OF MONTANA

VOL. V No. 18

MAY 4, 1925

*Walsh made the cover of* Time *magazine for May 4, 1925, when his Senate hearings broke open the Teapot Dome Scandal.*

**Senator Thomas Walsh was Montana's crusader against corruption.** The press hailed him as "the first man in history who is worth a billion dollars to his own government in his own lifetime."

Elected in 1912, the stern and righteous Senator Walsh was an uncompromising Democrat with a fierce reputation for ethical behavior. Historian David Stratton described him as a "gut Puritan…who combined party loyalty with a strict personal morality."

Walsh declared: "The one great, all-embracing political problem before the American people is the preservation of our institutions from falling wholly into the hands of…wealth [and]…degenerating into a sordid plutocracy."

### THE *NEW YORK SUN* SAID:

*"No wise…politician is likely to go to Walsh…looking for special favors. It would be like asking the Statue of Civic Virtue for a chew of tobacco."*

During the infamous Teapot Dome Scandal of the 1920s, crooked businessmen offered hefty bribes to high-ranking Harding Administration officials. Walsh spearheaded an investigation. It dominated national headlines, exposing what historian Robert Cherny dubbed the "greatest and most sensational scandal in the history of American politics." Walsh's twenty-five-month prosecution resulted in jail time for Interior Secretary Albert Fall—the first acting cabinet officer ever imprisoned for a felony.

Walsh became one of America's most respected politicians during the "Roaring Twenties."

In 1933, Franklin Delano Roosevelt named Walsh as his attorney general, but Walsh died while en route to accept nomination.

*Robert Yellowtail in his nineties.*

# ROBERT YELLOWTAIL

**Crow statesmen Robert Yellowtail spent a lifetime challenging the most powerful government on earth.**

This "20th Century Warrior" was born in 1889 in Lodge Grass. He attended reservation boarding schools and eventually earned a law degree. Yellowtail recalled: "I was disgusted with the way Indian affairs was being administered in Washington. I said to myself, 'I'm going to make this my life's work...and defend the Indians.'"

In 1910, Montana Senator Thomas Walsh suggested opening Crow Reservation lands to homesteaders. Yellowtail launched a seven-year battle to preserve his homeland—and won.

Yellowtail testified before Congress: "You have not one law that permits us to think free, act free, expand free, and decide free...I am here...to advocate the proposition [of citizenship] for the American Indian who is still in bondage as a political slave...an intellectual serf ..." Five years later, in June of 1924, Congress finally granted the first Americans the right to vote.

As the Crow Nation's first native superintendent, Yellowtail built the tribe's first hospital, stocked reservation lands with Yellowstone Park bison, and resurrected the Crow Fair. Yellowtail eventually became superintendent of the Bureau of Indian Affairs—a position he held for eleven years, longer than anyone before or since.

### WRITER CONSTANCE POTEN SUMMED UP YELLOWTAIL'S CAREER:

*"He seized the opportunity to return culture, pride, and a land-based economy to his people...He spent a lifetime fighting on the modern battlefield, a new warrior to the last."*

*John W. "Brick" Breeden*

# THE GOLDEN BOBCATS

**In the 1920s, Bozeman's Montana State Golden Bobcats were college basketball's "wonder team."**

Sportswriter Rial Cummings described them as: "perfectly suited to the Jazz Age: stylish and frenetic."

The Golden Bobcats pioneered the "fast break," gaining national attention with their thrilling full-court passes and snappy backward tosses. Historian Ellis Roberts Parry noted that they: "revolutionize(d) the game…by averaging over sixty points per game when most teams at the time scored in the high twenties or low thirties."

### THE *MIAMI NEWS* DUBBED MONTANA STATE:

*"The point-and-a-half per minute team," adding: "[this] seems about the human maximum unless a couple of howitzers are installed to fire the shots."*

Standouts "Cat" Thompson, "Brick" Breeden and Max Worthington, racked up a 102-11 record between 1926 and 1929. Their aggressive style of "racehorse basketball" won the Golden Bobcats three straight Rocky Mountain Conference titles. One year they outscored their opponents by more than a thousand points to become Collegiate National Champions.

One sportswriter noted: "All Montana was 'nuts' about their Bobcats, and so was the nation. Tremendous crowds [paid]…fantastic prices…for tickets to see them perform their feats…with a basketball."

The Helms Athletic Foundation named the 1929 Golden Bobcats as college basketball's top team of the first half of the twentieth century. They are enshrined today in MSU's athletic Hall of Fame, Brick Breeden Fieldhouse, and Max Worthington Arena.

Boots, the antelope, pet of the Big Elk Ranch, dressed in his little pack outfit, ready to start on a Rabbit and Pheasant hunt with his owner and trainer, Courtland Du Rand.

*DuRand never missed an opportunity for publicity.*

# COURTLAND DuRAND

**Martinsdale cowboy Courtland DuRand was Montana's dude ranching, game farming, and circus showman.**

In the 1920s, DuRand stocked his property with elk, bison, mountain goats, bighorn sheep, deer and antelope. This was America's first game farm—a quirky dude ranch zoo advertising horseback rides, trout fishing, western ambiance, and something new: domesticated "wild" animals.

Dressing like a drug-store cowboy, DuRand, in the words of biographer Lee Rostad: "bore that man-of-the-world air, suave and confident." The *Billings Gazette* called him: "a self-promoter par excellence." In rodeo parades, DuRand pranced his elk-drawn buggy past crowds. Clients flocked to what he billed as "the largest private game preserve in the nation," his Big Elk Ranch.

Tourists witnessed wild animal parades, rode saddle-clad elk and black-tail deer, took trained antelope on mountain pack trips, and marveled at haltered bison-calf yard pets.

DuRand's summer highlight was the "Wild Game Water Rodeo." From bleachers overlooking an artificial lake, people viewed trick ropers, a waterslide for horses, and bikini-clad bulldoggers.

### THE *MEAGHER COUNTY NEWS* REPORTED:

*"One elk was lassoed, and it pulled a rowboat with two passengers."*

Railroad representative Ed Bowers described the heart-pounding finale: "With a clattering roar, like the sound of a fast freight train through a covered bridge, a 2000-pound buffalo charges up the ramp and plunges forty feet into the lake below."

In 1951, a bull elk gored the 71-year-old DuRand in the stomach, abruptly ending his dude ranch days. He died four years later.

*The Bozeman Canning Company building advertised "peas that please."*

*This sheet-music artist seemed to confuse Bozeman's early Sweet-Pea Carnival (1906–1913) with a Mardi Gras celebration. When the modern Sweet Pea Festival (1977–present) was founded, its name purposefully referred back to the historical Carnival.*

# PEA CAPITAL OF THE NATION

**Montana's Gallatin Valley was once the "Pea Capital of the Nation."**

In 1911, studies confirmed nitrogen-rich legumes had potential as a profitable cash crop, animal fodder, and soil nutrient. The following year, the *Bozeman Daily Chronicle* reported: "the seed pea industry of the United States centers in the Gallatin Valley." The region raised 75 percent of the nation's crop.

During World War I, investors formed the Bozeman Canning Company. Marketed as "peas that please"; their company's "Gallatin Valley" and "Bridger Canyon" brands sold millions of cans across the nation.

Farmers shucked peas right in the field, then immediately shipped them to the canning plant by truck or rail. Cannery worker Louis Uhlrich recalled: "The [same] day" that workers brought the peas in from the vines "they had to be canned, or else they would sour…It was hard work, but you made a lot of money."

In the fall, women at seed pea houses removed insects, pebbles, and deformed legumes from an endless conveyor belt flow, sorting "as high as 120 pounds just by hand in a week's time."

### DURING THE GREAT DEPRESSION, DELLA DOYLE REMEMBERED:

*Seed companies "wouldn't allow anyone to work if their husband was working." Seed-house women "kept a lot of people from going hungry in those days."*

During the 1950s, larger West Coast operations and a terrible bacterial blight delivered fatal blows to the Gallatin Valley pea industry.

*Josephine Doody shows off her undoubtedly illegal catch.*

# JOSEPHINE DOODY

**Josephine Doody was "the Bootleg Lady of Glacier Park."**

She hailed from Georgia and had killed a man in Colorado while working as a dance hall girl. In 1890, now a fugitive, she landed in the seedy railroad town of McCarthyville, atop Marias Pass. From there, the *Missoulian* reported: "her legend [grew]…in Faulknerian proportions." Historian Ellen Baumler called her "a woman even more notorious than Calamity Jane" for "unlike Calamity, the events of her life are not disputed."

Her homesteading future husband, Dan, helped the foul-mouthed Doody survive opium addiction by tying her to a mule and dragging her to his remote 160-acre spread on the Middle Fork Flathead River. The couple used trained Airedales to trap fur-bearers and hunt mountain lions. Glacier National Park, created by Congress in 1910, surrounded their isolated homestead.

Dan worked as a park ranger…until he was fired for "excessive poaching." When he died, Josephine set up a backcountry moonshine still, fired by wood pilfered unapologetically from "her" park. At one point she hadn't seen another woman for seven years.

During Prohibition, her high-octane hooch became a favorite for thirsty Great Northern railroaders. They'd blast their train whistle once for each quart they wanted Josephine to row across the river.

Despite periodic clashes with nosy officials, Josephine ran whiskey from her cat-infested homestead until 1931. She died of pneumonia five years later, at age eighty-two.

### AUTHOR JOHN FRALEY WROTE:

*"She lived in the wilderness and she lived off the wilderness...She lived free."*

*Pretty Shield left a legacy of what the change to reservation life was like for her Crow people.*

# PRETTY SHIELD

**At age seventy-four, the Crow medicine woman Pretty Shield told her story to author Frank Bird Linderman.** Using sign language and an interpreter, she related what scholars have called "perhaps the first record of female Native American life."

Born in 1856, Pretty Shield was—according to Professor Hertha D. Wong: "a lively, intelligent woman, with a playful sense of humor and a survivor's spirit." She provided a detailed account of pre-reservation life in Montana when, her "people's hearts were…as light as breath feathers."

Pretty Shield recalled: "The happiest days of my life were spent following the buffalo herds over our beautiful country…I believed I had everything that was good on this world."

As a child, Pretty Shield kicked balls stuffed with antelope hair and raced down snowy hillsides on sleds made of buffalo ribs. Later she described her marriage, childbirth, and child-rearing practices, sacred healing practices, and the first time she saw white people. She called them *Beta-awk-a-wah-cha* or Sits on the Water, because they were seen in canoes.

Pretty Shield mourned the loss of the buffalo and the advent of reservation life, stating: "Our hearts were like stones…We began to stay in one place, and to grow lazy and sicker all the time."

### PRIOR TO HER DEATH IN 1944, PRETTY SHIELD ADMITTED:

*"The times have changed so fast that they have left me behind…I am walking in the dark…I belong to that other world."*

*The 1935 Helena quakes downed this Nabisco plant on Boulder Avenue.*

# THE CAPITAL QUAKES OF 1935

**On an October night in 1935, a severe, 6.2 scale earthquake slammed Montana's capital city.**

Resident Gil Alexander wrote: "Violently, uncontrollably, Helena rocked with the shuddering earth…The ground rolled like waves, bricks and mortar fell, buildings swayed, roofs fell in…"

Businessman Fred Buck recalled: "[It was like] being jostled about like a lone marble in a tomato can…Old Mother Earth reminded me of a dog full of fleas shaking himself to get rid of the dirt."

### A BOZEMAN PAPER WROTE:

*The capital is now called simply "Lena," because the quake shook "the Hell out of it."*

A couple weeks later, just as people started to rebuild, another massive tremor hit. Historian C.R. Anderson wrote: "People…jumped to places of safety…[and] awaited the end…But…[i]nstead the trembling increased, the violence became terrific, walls crashed which had been weakened by so many previous shakes…"

More than 1200 aftershocks rattled Helena in the next few months. The quakes killed four, injured dozens, and destroyed some 300 buildings.

The *Boston Post* reported: "Living there must be a nightmare. One can get used to just about anything except the solid earth shaking constantly. Only the pioneering spirit of the early founders that is still retained by the present generation keeps the city from becoming a wilderness. If Congressional Medals of Honor were given to groups for outstanding courage this community would deserve one."

*Aerial view of the boom-town of Wheeler*

**During the Great Depression, Wheeler was the "King of Montana boomtowns."**

Named for U.S. Senator Burton K. Wheeler, it was one of eighteen colorful shantytowns that sprang up to house men constructing the Fort Peck Dam—one of the New Deal Era's largest public works projects.

At its peak, Wheeler was a rowdy metropolis of nearly 5,000 young, gritty, migratory dam workers.

### ONE RESIDENT WROTE:

*"Here we are out where there is nothing but thistles, black widow spiders, ticks, rattlesnakes, and heat. We're living in pasteboard boxes and eatin' dirt, with nothing to do when were not working but guzzle beer and wake up with a headache."*

Wheeler boasted twenty all-night saloons. In 1936, famed "roving correspondent" Ernie Pyle dubbed it "the wildest wild-west town in North America," writing that "(e)xcept for the autos, it is a genuine throwback… to Tombstone and Dodge City…"

Casino owner Ruby Smith, "the Queen of Wheeler Night Life," declared: "These boys and girls are having their fun while they can…They know it won't last forever. It will all be over here in a year or two, then we'll all drift along."

When the seven-year Fort Peck project finished in 1940, Wheeler and most of Montana's other dam-building boomtowns dried up. Today, only the incorporated towns of Glasgow, Fort Peck, and Nashua survive.

*Wreckage of the* Olympian *below the destroyed Saugus trestle.*

# CUSTER CREEK TRAIN WRECK OF 1938

*Life* **magazine called it "the worst American Train Wreck" in fifty years.**

On a day in June 1938, eastern Montana experienced "a cloudburst of unprecedented proportions." A raging, thirty-foot wall of water swamped Custer Creek, damaging the Saugus railroad trestle west of Miles City.

Later that night, the Milwaukee Road's eleven-car passenger flyer—the *Olympian*—was racing full throttle toward the bridge. On board: 165 passengers. One account noted: "There was no water on the track—nothing to warn the crewmen of approaching disaster."

The engine and five cars roared over the collapsing bridge. Custer Creek had swept away the center span. Two cars dropped into the seething waters. The *Rochester Daily Times* reported: "Their weight, multiplied by their plunge...jerked the locomotive...into the air and backward—like the tip of a lashing whip."

Witnesses described "a tangled mass...broken like an eggshell." Seventeen-year-old Evelyn Jenson clung to a tangled trestle fragment for hours before being pulled to safety.

### EVELYN JENSON RECALLED:

*"I heard a lot of screaming...I saw the engineer and the fireman...burnt to a crisp. I saw some awful things."*

At dawn, rescuers pulled lifeless, pajama-clad bodies from sunken, silt-filled sleeping cars. Some corpses were found 100 miles downstream.

Forty-seven died and seventy-five were injured in Montana's worst rail disaster.

*Wilderness-protection pioneer Bob Marshall was an unprepossessing man who ignored his health problems.*

# BOB MARSHALL

**If ever there was a man for whom a wilderness should be named, it was Bob Marshall.**

The Forest Service assigned the 24-year-old Marshall to Missoula's Northern Rocky Mountain Experiment Station. There, he regularly explored Montana's backcountry on marathon thirty- to forty-mile-per-day hikes, and concluded: "Wilderness is melting away like some last snow bank on some south-facing mountainside during a hot afternoon in June."

In the years that followed, historian Roderick Nash observes, Marshall became "a legend in his own time: prodigious hiker, explorer of the earth's far corners, best-selling author, millionaire, socialist, Ph.D.—one of the most colorful figures in forest history."

In Marshall's time, most Americans saw the land as merely a supplier of natural resources. For Marshall, it was much more. He wrote: "[I]n a world overrun by split-second schedules, physical certainty, and man-made superficiality," it is necessary to preserve a "certain precious value of the timeless, the mysterious and the primordial..."

## IN MARSHALL'S VIEW:

*"The enjoyment of solitude, complete independence, and the beauty of undefiled panoramas is absolutely essential to happiness."*

While serving as the Forest Service's chief of recreation and lands, Marshall added 5.4 million acres to the nation's wilderness system. In 1934, he helped found the Wilderness Society.

Marshall's convictions were strong, but his heart weak. He died in 1939 at just thirty-eight. Two years later, the federal government created Montana's million-acre Bob Marshall Wilderness Area.

*Alice Greenough rodeoed from 1919 to 1954.*

# ALICE GREENOUGH

**Alice Greenough, Montana's cowgirl extraordinaire, used to say that she was "born liberated" in 1902.**

"I've done it all," she declared. "I rode bulls. I rode broncs. I trick rode. They used to call me 'The queen of the Bronc Riders'…"

Greenough grew up ranching near Red Lodge. Drunken cowpokes dared Greenough to take her first competition ride—a bronc in the 1919 Forsyth Rodeo. Soon she was executing cartwheels and handstands from the backs of galloping horses in Jack King's Wild West Show.

### JOURNALIST BETSEY COHEN REPORTED:

*"[She] busted broncs and busted ranks in the macho world of rodeoing…She was, hands down, the first rodeo queen."*

She performed throughout North America, Europe, and Australia. In England, she took tea with the Queen. In Spain, unarmed, she rode fighting bulls into arenas, presenting them to matadors.

Alice Greenough won four World Champion Saddle Bronc Rider titles. She retired from rodeo in 1954, but still worked as a trick rider and stunt double in Hollywood films and television until she was 80. She was the first inductee into the Cowgirl Hall of Fame. *Sports Illustrated* called her Montana's best female athlete.

Alice Greenough died in 1995 at age 93. Her *New York Times* obituary remembered "[Alice] was always at home on a horse. If it was bucking, so much the better."

*In the pristine General Motors test kitchens, cooking seems an easy, delightful process.*

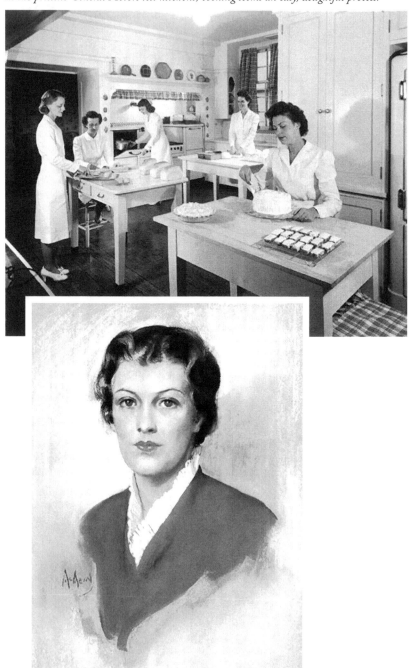

*Advertising's (and General Mills') original "Betty Crocker,"*
*in 1936.*

# JANETTE KELLEY

**Janette Kelley helped form America's first all-American home-maker, Betty Crocker.** Born in Deer Lodge, Montana, in 1894, she attended Bozeman's Montana State College, where classmates voted her "the best-natured, jolliest, fattest and best-liked Junior on the hill."

About 1921, Kelley hired on with the Minneapolis-based company now known as General Mills. She established the corporation's first test kitchens and cookbooks, promoting their product "Gold Medal Flour."

When baking enquiries flooded in, ad agents created "Betty Crocker"—a folksy, fictional persona to personalize responses from Kelley's fifty-woman staff.

The *Encyclopedia of Food and Culture* called Betty Crocker "a cultural icon…[who] has helped generations of American women…deal with… food scarcity during the Depression and World War II, a renewed emphasis on homemaking in the postwar years, and the increasing sophistication of American taste."

Recipes from Kelley's kitchens were everywhere—in newspaper columns, radio and TV spots, and the still bestselling *Betty Crocker Picture Cookbooks*. Among the innovations was "the cake discovery of the century"— the light, butter-rich sponge cake dubbed "the chiffon."

## WRITER JEREMY SMITH OBSERVED:

*"Kelley's face and name remained anonymous, but her influence was enormous."*

In 1945 *Fortune Magazine* dubbed Betty Crocker the second-most-popular woman in America. Since number one was Eleanor Roosevelt, Crocker was called "the First Lady of Food."

Kelley died in February 1958. She is buried in Deer Lodge.

*Early studio glamour shot of Myrna Loy.*

*Loy wisecracked with screen husband William Powell through several "Thin Man" films.*

# MYRNA LOY

**With her almond-shaped eyes and dignified manner, Myrna Loy was a goddess in the golden age of the silver screen.** Ed Sullivan crowned her "The Queen of Hollywood."

Loy was born Myrna Adele Williams in 1905 near Radersburg and was raised in Helena. She was thirteen when her family moved to Los Angeles. She changed her name and took up acting.

Loy played femme fatales in silent movies. She landed a part in 1927's landmark *The Jazz Singer*, but struggled to get beyond her vamp typecasting.

### DIRECTOR JOHN FORD PROCLAIMED:

*"Wouldn't you know, the kid they pick to play tramps is the only good girl in Hollywood?"*

Between 1934 and 1947, Loy remade her image. Co-starring with Clark Gable, Cary Grant, and others, she came to embody the perfect American wife—wholesome, sympathetic, and funny. Men-Must-Marry-Myrna Clubs formed. Actor Jimmy Stewart joked: "I shall only marry Myrna Loy!"

Loy demurred: "Some perfect wife I am. I've been…divorced four times, have no children, and can't boil an egg."

Journalist Tony Rogers described Loy as "a woman as comfortable with the political world as with the glittery avenues of Hollywood." She was the first big star to publicly campaign for civil rights and first-amendment freedoms during the McCarthy years.

Myrna Loy died in 1993, two years after Helena's Myrna Loy Center for the Performing Arts was named in her honor.

*Butte's U.S. Senator James Murray supported New Deal programs that included Social Security and federal dam-building in Montana.*

# SENATOR JAMES MURRAY (PART 1)

**"I would rather die a martyr to a righteous cause than to enjoy the luxury and happiness of a thousand years on a sun-blessed fairy isle..."**—that's U.S. Senator James E. Murray, a quiet, now largely forgotten politician whom Helena newspaper editor Harry Billings called "the greatest Montanan ever sent to the nation's capitol."

Murray was an Irish Catholic Democrat from Butte. During the Great Depression he voiced "one hundred per-cent support" for President Franklin Roosevelt's New Deal and in 1934 won a seat in the Senate.

A steadfast champion for the less fortunate, Murray sought to expand Social Security, provide free medical care for the aged, and increase aid to education. He defended unions and was an early advocate for a national healthcare law.

Murray drafted Hawaii and Alaska statehood bills, then guided them to passage. He introduced legislation to create ten new national parks and brought about construction of Montana's Canyon Ferry, Yellowtail, Hungry Horse, and Libby dams.

Murray served longer than any previous Montana Senator. He resigned in 1961 and died in Butte less than three months later.

### BIOGRAPHERS JOHN AND CATHERINE MORRISON CONCLUDED:

*"For Jim Murray, the battle for social justice was not a cause for compromise. In a most remarkable way, he resisted intimidation...and survived for more than a quarter century as an advocate for the common man."*

# SENATOR JAMES MURRAY (PART 2)

**While most Americans remained silent during Hitler's holocaust, Democratic U.S. Senator James Murray of Montana spoke out in defense of the Jews.**

Historian Rafael Medoff wrote: "Murray had little to gain—and much to lose—by taking an interest in rescuing European Jewish refugees [who then constituted]...barely one third of one percent of the state's population."

Prior to Pearl Harbor, most Montanans were isolationists. Burton K. Wheeler—the state's influential senior senator—campaigned against intervention. Others, like Republican Congressman Jacob Thorkelson, railed *against* "communistic Jews" and "Jewish international financiers" from the floor of the U.S. House of Representatives.

But Murray—defying all political logic—condemned Hitler as a "ruthless, dangerous maniac." He was among the first in Washington to condemn the Holocaust, calling it "a terrible problem which has been too long evaded..."

FDR' preferred "rescue through victory," but Murray demanded saving "the helpless Jews of Europe, who are facing a purposeful annihilation on a scale the world has never seen..."

### MURRAY WARNED:

*"We dare not wait any longer...for every day of postponement means death to thousands of innocent victims...If we wait until the war is won, there may be only corpses left to enjoy victory."*

Murray helped convince FDR to establish the War Refugee Board, liberating 200,000 Jews in the final months of the war. Then Murray again took the lead, advocating for a "free and democratic Jewish state in Palestine."

In 1948, the United Nations General assembly approved the creation of the modern state of Israel.

*World War II refugees trekked across the countryside with all their belongings, seeking welcoming havens.*

*Spotted Wolf, in uniform, posed with Potawatami friend Celia Mix for a magazine article.*

# MINNIE SPOTTED WOLF

**Private Minnie Spotted Wolf was the first Native American woman to enlist in the United States Marine Corps.**

Born at Heart Butte in 1923, Spotted Wolf was a member of the Blackfeet Tribe. She worked on her father's ranch, cutting fence posts, driving a two-ton truck, and breaking horses.

After Pearl Harbor, Spotted Wolf became one of more than 250,000 women to join the military. A recruiter told her "the war is not really for women." Spotted Wolf enlisted anyway.

Her daughter, Gerry England, recalled: "[She] really wanted…to serve her country. Her brother had died, and she knew nobody else in the family would be able to serve."

Promotional magazines and newspapers—even a full-color comic spread in a girl's magazine entitled "One Little Indian"—featured Spotted Wolf and her patriotic story.

### THE MAGAZINE BEGAN:

*"20-year-old Minnie Spotted Wolf, full-blooded Blackfoot Indian, did a man's job before the war. Now she's taking a man's place in the United States Marines."*

England said, "A few people picked on her for being an Indian, but… Mom was proud of who she was. She wasn't in the military just for herself, but for the Indian people. She wanted others to know who she was and where she came from."

Spotted Wolf received an honorable discharge in 1947. Afterward, she married, had four children, and worked as an elementary teacher for twenty-nine years. When she died in 1988, she was buried in her uniform.

*Members of the Devil's Brigade shelter behind a haystack while receiving orders during the Anzio, Italy, invasion of January 22, 1944.*

# THE DEVIL'S BRIGADE

**In 1942, Fort Harrison near Helena became home to the First Special Service Force, the FSSF—a top-secret, World War II commando unit nicknamed "the Devil's Brigade."**

This elite group of Canadians and Americans completed heart-pounding winter missions behind enemy lines. Recruiters promised them "a short and exciting life."

Veteran Roy Hudson recalled: "We were the first 'Green Beret' outfit. We did it all—we were paratroopers, demolition experts, mountaineers, ski troopers and an amphibious landing force."

Journalist Charles Hillinger wrote: "Many had been cowboys, trappers, lumberjacks and longshoremen. While training in the mountains of Montana, they slept in snow without blankets to prepare themselves for hardships."

Once in action, the FSSF never failed a combat mission. Brigade members blackened their faces for midnight raids and captured 30,000 enemy prisoners. Calling cards placed on dead Nazis warned: "The worst is yet to come."

In the Alps, the unit scaled a 3,000 foot cliff—at night—to capture a heavily fortified German stronghold that had kept the Allies from taking Rome.

### A DIARY FOUND NEAR A SLAIN GERMAN OFFICER OBSERVED:

*"The black devils are all around us...we never hear them."*

Three quarters of the "Devil's Brigade" were killed or wounded in combat. Officials disbanded the unit in December 1944.

*Joe Medicine Crow sang and drummed in the White House after receiving the Presidential Medal of Freedom.*

# JOSEPH MEDICINE CROW

**In 2014 Joseph Medicine Crow was the oldest living member of the Crow tribe.** A while back, author Catherine Clarke Fox declared "[He] has walked in both the Indian world and the white man's world for 93 years."

Born in 1913 near Lodge Grass, Medicine Crow was the first member of his tribe to attend college. World War II interrupted his graduate studies in anthropology at the University of Southern California. Said Medicine Crow: "My Uncle had other plans for me…Uncle Sam, that is."

As a 103rd Infantry Division scout, Medicine Crow wore war paint beneath his uniform and a sacred eagle feather beneath his helmet. He called it "my strong Indian medicine…[it's what] brought me back."

### IN WORLD WAR II, MEDICINE CROW COMPLETED TASKS THAT WOULD MAKE HIM THE LAST CROW WAR CHIEF:

*He touched a living enemy, disarmed a foe in combat, led a successful war party, and stole horses from German officers. Riding off, he sang a Crow honor song.*

Historian Peter Nabokov deemed him: "Remarkable as an example of particular tribal continuity…[He] represents the thousands of Indian soldiers whose bravery against the Germans and the Japanese was part of an inherited warrior code."

Joseph Medicine Crow was awarded a Bronze Star and France's Legion of Honor. On August 12, 2009, he received America's highest civilian honor, the Presidential Medal of Freedom.

*Montana's Jungleers, "island hopping" toward Japan, fight on Wakde Island, New Guinea, May 16, 1944.*

# THE MONTANA JUNGLEERS

**Montana's National Guard endured some of the most vicious fighting of World War II.**

Officially, they were the 163rd regiment of the 41st Infantry Division. The 41st was the first American Division sent overseas after Pearl Harbor, and the first trained in jungle warfare, earning them the nickname "The Jungleers." They spent forty-five months overseas, longer than any other Division.

The "green hell" in the South Pacific was a far cry from Big Sky Country. Tropical New Guinea featured 100-degree temperatures, steep, rain-drenched mountains, and crocodile-filled swamps.

Troops crawled through twisting wild boar paths defended by Japanese snipers. Malaria, dengue fever, and typhus plagued the soldiers. Kalispell guardsman Sergeant Leslie Slyter said: "Everything that lit on you…made you sick. Everything you touched cut you. Everything you drank gave you dysentery…and the very worst of it was malnutrition…Fear was present all of the time, but you couldn't show it."

### SERGEANT ED HULA OF COLUMBIA FALLS REMEMBERED:

*"At first it seemed good to be going to war with longtime friends. But I soon wished that I were in an outfit of strangers. It was terribly hard…to see close friends struck down in action…"*

Three hundred sixty Montana National Guardsmen died in the South Pacific, and 1,491 others were wounded. But the highly decorated "Jungleers" earned acclaim for their important role in defeating the Japanese in the South Pacific.

*Joseph Kinsey Howard, comfortable in his Great Falls apartment*

# JOSEPH KINSEY HOWARD

**"Montana has lived the life of America, on a reduced scale and at breakneck speed.** Its history has been bewilderingly condensed, a kaleidoscopic newsreel, unplotted and unplanned…" Speaking was Montana's uncompromising journalist-historian Joseph Kinsey Howard.

The dashing, Clark Gable–like Howard settled in Great Falls in 1919 and quickly found work as a journalist. His expressive and engaging style soon caught the attention of national magazines like *The Nation*, *Harper's*, *Time* and *Life*.

Howard's masterpiece was the 1943 classic, *Montana: High Wide and Handsome*—an epic work the *Great Falls Tribune* called years later "a 'must-read' even now…" In it, Howard artfully "championed the Native American, the worker, the land, and the community long before they became fashionable topics." He also boldly confronted the corporate giants that he felt unfairly exploited Montana, making it what he described as a "plundered province."

When, in 1947, the colossal Anaconda Company sent Howard a $500 payoff to write some corporate leaning articles about Butte, Howard refused the offer, writing: "I'd hate to sound like the chaste maiden nobly spurning a mink coat…It is just that…I could not retain any respect for myself as writer if I accepted it…"

Though he died of a heart attack in 1951 at just forty-five years old, Joseph Kinsey Howard remains one of Montana's most gifted and influential authors.

### NOVELIST A.B. GUTHRIE CALLED HIM:

*"Montana's conscience…the greatest Montanan of our time, perhaps of any time."*

*Cooper looks "actorish" in this post–World War II studio portrait.*

# GARY COOPER

**The *Helena Independent Record* once proclaimed: "It is almost inconceivable to think of Gary Cooper...as being born in Brooklyn, South Pasadena, or anywhere other than Helena."**

Frank James "Gary" Cooper was one of Hollywood's greatest box office attractions. He was born in 1901 in Montana's capital city. His father was a state Supreme Court Justice. On the family ranch near Craig, Cooper worked cattle and rode horses. After being expelled from Helena High School—for smearing Limburger cheese on heat radiators—he moved to Bozeman and graduated from Gallatin County High School in 1922.

Cooper drew political cartoons and drove an open-air tourist bus in Yellowstone, but his cowboy pedigree brought him success in Tinseltown. He began in westerns as a stuntman, falling off horses. By 1939, he had become Hollywood's leading man and America's top wage earner.

"Coop" made more than 100 films. In many he played a steadfast, self-reliant cowboy hero.

### COOPER ONCE CONFESSED:

*"When I do a western, I don't feel actorish."*

One reporter called Cooper: "A true westerner in appearance—lean, leggy, loping, leathery, his sharp eyes surrounded with lines from too much squinting at far horizons through sun and wind and dust; his speech careful, leisurely and unemotional."

Gary Cooper was nominated five times for a Best Actor Oscar and won twice, for *Sergeant York* and *High Noon*. He died of lung cancer in 1961.

*McGill at her Gallatin Valley ranch*

**Compassionate, dedicated, and barely five feet tall, Doctor Caroline McGill cast a giant shadow on the Treasure State.**

Born on a Missouri farm in 1879, McGill became Montana's first pathologist and earned a medical degree from Johns Hopkins. She settled in Butte, informing her family: "I'll have to work my head off to make good...But it's all done, and I have to let her rip."

The good doctor made house calls to crude miners' shacks, treating tuberculosis, alcoholism, syphilis, and "black lung." Impoverished patients traded family heirlooms for her services. In time, McGill's remarkable antique collection became the nucleus of Bozeman's Museum of the Rockies.

Mining City resident Linda Burgess called McGill "a most amazing person...slight and extremely active...she can out walk any person in Butte."

### COMMENTING ON HER HECTIC LIFE, McGILL SAID:

*"I do not believe a woman can be a full-time doctor, a full-time wife, and a full-time mother and do all three well... I choose medicine."*

Doctor McGill loved the scenic Gallatin Canyon, and it was there that she became a devoted conservationist. She acquired the 320 Dude Ranch and placed thousands of acres in conservation easements. The Montana Wilderness Association named McGill its first lifelong member.

Before her death in 1959, Montana State College (now University) awarded McGill an honorary degree for her "lifelong service to Montana both in the field of medicine and her interest in its resources."

*Kirby Grant in costume for his television show* Sky King Montana Historical
Society Research Center Photograph Archives, Helena

# KIRBY "SKY KING" GRANT

**Montana native Kirby Grant was television's Sky King, "America's favorite flying cowboy."**

Born in Butte in 1911 and raised in Helena, Grant had bit parts beside the likes of Henry Fonda before gaining fame in the popular 1950s television show *Sky King*. Born as a radio broadcast in 1946, the series featured Schuyler "Sky" King, a World War II naval aviator turned crime-fighting rancher who soared "from out of the clear blue of the Western sky" chasing black-hatted jewel smugglers, bank robbers and gangsters in his agile twin-engine Cessna.

### JOURNALIST JERRY LIPS WROTE:

*"The episodes were filled with excitement and danger. The fantastic flying sequences made the series a hit."*

Aviation writer Christopher Freeze added: "Mention the name Sky King to just about all pilots over fifty and chances are a smile will come to their faces as they begin to tell you about how…they watched the show…and dreamed of flying someday."

Missoula resident Kay Whitlock admitted: "[Grant] wasn't my idea of a cowboy…[But Sky King] was this amalgam of Western and Modernity …You could see what you'd seen all your life, but from a different perspective…You could fly in and out of danger…The plane was a doorway to imagination."

In 1985, the 73-year-old Grant died in a car wreck while traveling to see a space shuttle *Challenger* launch at Cape Canaveral. He's buried in Missoula.

*"Sister Buckskin" rides in a Rocky Boy Reservation parade.*

# SISTER PROVIDENCIA TOLAN

**Sister Providencia Tolan was known to native peoples as "Sister Buckskin."**

She was born in 1904 in Anaconda. As an adult, she grew concerned with the plight of urban Indians, displaced from the Treasure State's reservations to "Hill 57" near the garbage dumps of Great Falls.

To Chippewa-Cree leader Edward Eagleman she was "[a] fearless and eloquent sister, and…one of the best informed persons in the United States on the Indians' economic problem."

Tolan educated Indian children, tirelessly sought donations of food and clothing, and chided those who "resorted to an ostrich-like attitude…"

Great Falls resident Jack Albanese remembered her constant motion "from the hospital to the city jail, to the county jail, to the bars…in search of and on behalf of human beings in need."

When the federal government tried to "terminate" its tribal obligations during the 1950s, Tolan led the protest.

### TOLAN DECLARED:

*"I warn the dinosaurs who still think the Indians are 'things' to get pushed around… move out of the way."*

Congressman Lee Metcalf called her "a sparkplug and a catalyst" for reform. To Senator James Murray she "spoke the conscience of those of us who are concerned with Indian welfare."

Sister Providencia died in 1989. Father Robert Fox called Tolan a "joyful friend who came charging into our lives," who would "make the sparks fly and help us to hear the thunder roar in the land of the Shining Mountains."

*Young Montie Montana shows off his riding and roping skills.*

# MONTIE MONTANA

**Trick roping superstar Montie Montana often said: "If you can't do it on horseback, it probably ain't worth doin'."**

Born 1910, Owen Harlan Mickel grew up in Wolf Point. He recalled: "I saw a fellow spin a rope…when I was about 6 years old. So [I]…decided to give it a try."

At the 1925 Miles City rodeo, an arena announcer forgot Mickel's name, so just said: "Here's Montie from Montana." The moniker stuck: "Montie Montana."

One of his more extraordinary feats was roping five running horses—all mounted by pretty cowgirls—with a single toss of a long lasso. He took his horse, Poncho Rex, to the top of the Empire State Building "to let him get a look at the Big Apple."

Montana appeared in countless movies as a stunt double for stars like John Wayne and Roy Rogers. The *Los Angeles Daily News* christened him "One Of The Last 'White Hats' Of Hollywood Westerns."

In 1953, Montana grabbed national headlines—and miffed Secret Service agents—when he roped President Eisenhower as a gag during his inaugural parade. Over the years, Montana made more than sixty showy appearances astride a silver-saddled palomino in Pasadena's annual Tournament of Roses Parade.

Montie Montana died in 1998.

COWBOY FILM STAR GENE AUTRY DECLARED:

*"I was proud to call [him] my friend. He was a fine cowboy, a good man and undoubtedly the greatest trick roper of his time.'"*

*Johnson, at left, with Gary Cooper at the 1958 press conference announcing that her novel* The Hanging Tree, *starring Cooper, was to be filmed.* MANSFIELD LIBRARY, UNIVERSITY OF MONTANA–MISSOULA

# DOROTHY JOHNSON

**Though she lived in the twentieth century, award-winning author Dorothy Johnson lived and breathed the 1800s.**

Born in Iowa, Johnson was an infant when her family moved to Whitefish in 1913. She would study creative writing in Missoula, then start a sixty-year career penning tales of the wild west and its often-desperate occupants.

Three of her westerns became film classics: *The Hanging Tree*, starring fellow Montanan Gary Cooper; *The Man Who Shot Liberty Valance*, with John Wayne and Jimmy Stewart; and *A Man Called Horse*, with Richard Harris in the title role.

Her looks—a plump grandmother with Coke-bottle glasses—were deceiving. Writer Steve Smith called her "A witty, gritty little bobcat of a woman…[who] could think like a cowboy or trapper." Johnson kept a pistol nearby when writing.

### JOHNSON SAID:

*"There's something about a Colt .44 beside the typewriter that inspires me."*

Johnson wrote dozens of books, short stories, and articles. *Time* magazine compared her to Bret Harte and Mark Twain. Literary authority Richard Tyre described her style as "lean, unadorned and understated…reminiscent of Hemingway at his best."

Upon her death in 1984, film critic Les Benedict wrote: "Her ability to tell Western stories in new and different ways lifted her into the top echelon of modern Western writers…Dorothy Johnson was…one of Montana's true treasures."

She was inducted into the Gallery of Outstanding Montanans in the Montana Capitol in 2011.

*Gibson Dam on the Sun River receives the onslaught of the 1964 flood.*

# FLOOD OF 1964

**Sixteen inches of rain fell in just 48 hours on the Continental Divide on June 7 and 8, 1964.** Peaceful creeks became deadly, mile-wide rivers. Roughly 20 percent of the state was flooded.

The Blackfeet Reservation was hardest hit. On Birch Creek, the Swift Dam broke. Shelby radio announcer Bob Norris heard "a great cracking sound, like a giant thunder and lightening bolt," before "thousands of tons of cascading water roared...into the valley, snuffing out homes and lives in a matter of seconds."

### JOURNALIST HELEN WEST REPORTED THAT THE DAM'S RAGING TORRENT:

*"Reached a height of twenty to forty feet, sweeping all before it: trees, power lines, homes, cattle, horses and bodies of those who had no chance."*

Swollen rivers destroyed 265 homes, drowned thousands of acres of crop-land, tore out bridges and most of the roads on the Reservation. Thirty people died in the flood of 1964, all of them on the Blackfeet Reservation.

Floodwaters left thousands homeless and caused $62 million in damages. President Lyndon B. Johnson declared nine Montana counties a federal disaster area. The flood was the Treasure State's worst natural disaster on record.

One survivor put it this way: "At first, everyone was joking and happy about their narrow escapes. Then, when they were told they could go home, everyone realized that there were no homes to go to."

*Montana's long-time U.S. Senator, Mike Mansfield, made the cover of* Time *magazine, March 20, 1964, when he was working to pass the Civil Rights Act.*

# SENATE MAJORITY LEADER MIKE MANSFIELD

**Mike Mansfield was "Montana's gift to American statesmanship and to world diplomacy."**

Thin and tall, often described as Lincolnesque, Mansfield possessed what political consultant Marc Johnson called: "a rare combination of intelligence,…honesty, modesty and staying power…"

Mansfield represented Montana in Washington from 1942 to 1977. The Democrat was Senate Majority Leader for sixteen years—longer than anyone else in history.

Montana legislator Steve Dougherty observed: "[Mansfield] presided over a tempestuous body in a tumultuous period. Civil rights,…an Asian war turned to strife at home, a war on poverty,…a race to the moon and the resignation of a president, all hurtled forward under his hand."

Republican Senator Ted Stevens of Alaska called him "the best leader we ever had [in the U.S. Senate]."

Following service in the Senate, Mansfield served a twelve-year stint as U.S. Ambassador to Japan.

### A TOKYO NEWSPAPER DECLARED:

*"A giant walks among us."*

Mansfield once stated: "When I'm gone, I want to be forgotten." Chances of this are slim to none. Historian Dave Walter wrote: "[H]e dwarfs the legends and heroes with whom he has been cast on stages in both Montana and Washington, D.C.…In influence and example, Mike Mansfield has no 20th-century political equal."

Mike Mansfield died October 5, 2001.

*Lee Metcalf enjoying his beloved Montana outdoors, at Canyon Ferry on the Missouri River.*

# SENATOR LEE METCALF

**Democratic U.S. Senator Lee Metcalf was Montana's environmental champion.** The Stevensville native was a World War II veteran, state legislator, assistant attorney general, Montana Supreme Court justice, and, in 1952, Montana's congressman in the U.S. House of Representatives.

Metcalf called for elder health-care legislation a decade before the creation of Medicare. He earned the nickname "Mr. Education" as a leading supporter of the Elementary and Secondary Education Act. *Time* magazine dubbed him: "An archetypal Western populist."

After 1960, Metcalf served in the U.S. Senate, becoming a pioneer in conservation. Wisconsin Senator Gaylord Nelson recalled: "He was one of only a few national leaders who…[before it became fashionable or politically acceptable] spoke out strongly and repeatedly for…[environmental protection legislation.]"

Metcalf's "Save Our Streams" bill protected fish and wildlife from pesticides. He co-sponsored the Wilderness Act of 1964, then helped create Montana's Great Bear and Absaroka-Beartooth wilderness areas. Congressman Pat Williams concluded: "[He] preserve[d] the best of the West and in doing so he…changed the way we envisioned ourselves on the land."

## JOURNALIST DALE BURK WROTE:

*"Metcalf argued his cause—eloquently or bluntly as the case demanded—letting the chips fall where they might...[T]he little guy of this and future generations counted on him."*

When Metcalf died in 1978, the Sierra Club eulogized: "We shall not soon see his record of courage and commitment equaled." In his honor, Congress created Montana's Lee Metcalf Wilderness Area in 1983.

*McNally at the height of his baseball career*

# DAVE McNALLY

*Sports Illustrated* **named Dave McNally "Montana's Athlete of the Century."**

The Billings baseball great debuted with the Baltimore Orioles in 1962. Southpaw McNally and Hall-of-Famer Jim Palmer were part of one of baseball history's most formidable starting pitching rotations.

McNally and the Orioles dynasty played in four World Series between 1966 and 1971.

### MANAGER EARL WEAVER CALLED HIM:

*"An unbelievable competitor...He loved to set you up with a change, fool you with that tremendous curve and then throw the fastball by you...."*

McNally was a four-time 20-game winner. In 1968, he tied an American League pitching record with 17 straight wins, earning the moniker "Dave McLucky." He remains the only pitcher in Major League history to hit a World Series grand slam.

McNally once said: "[T]he proudest thing I have left from those days is the respect of my teammates...They knew when I went out there... I didn't leave anything on the bench...They got everything I had to give."

In 1975, McNally and Andy Messersmith challenged baseball's "reserve clause." They won a landmark victory establishing baseball's free-agent era. The case led to multimillion-dollar salaries and changed the face of pro sports.

Upon retirement in 1975, McNally returned to Billings and started an auto dealership with his brother. He died of lung cancer in 2002.

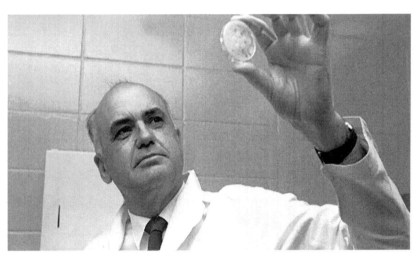

*In this posed picture, Hilleman repeated the examination of a Petrie dish done so many times in his career.*

# MAURICE HILLEMAN

**By the end of his pioneering life, Maurice Hilleman had became "the world's leading vaccinologist."**

Raised on a Miles City farm, Hilleman earned degrees in chemistry and microbiology from Bozeman's Montana State College in 1941.

At pharmaceutical giant Merck, Hilleman developed vaccines for mumps, measles, chickenpox, pneumonia, meningitis and other diseases. Dr. Hilleman described himself as a renegade.

Immunologist David M. Morens said: "Unlike many scientists who understand the leaf on the tree, he understood the whole forest...He...really was a big picture guy."

The *New York Times* concluded: "Much of modern preventive medicine is based on Hilleman's work, though he never received the public recognition of Salk...or Pasteur."

## THE *NEW YORK TIMES* WROTE:

*"He...probably saved more lives than any other scientist in the 20th century."*

Dr. Anthony Fauci, director of the National Institute of Allergy and Infectious Diseases, proclaimed: "Just one of his accomplishments would be enough to have made for a great scientific career. One can say without hyperbole that Maurice changed the world with his extraordinary contributions..."

In the 1970s Hilleman developed the first licensed vaccine against any viral cancer. His vaccines prevented deafness, blindness and permanent disabilities in millions of people. President Ronald Reagan presented Hilleman with the National Medal of Science, the nation's highest scientific honor.

# EVEL KNIEVEL

**Evel Knievel—America's greatest motorcycle showman—was the King of the Daredevils, the Godfather of Extreme Sports, and, by his own account: "The Last Gladiator in the New Rome."**

Ty van Hooydonk of the Motorcycle Industry Council called him: "the two-wheel equivalent of Elvis."

Born in Butte, Robert Craig Knievel mined copper until he was fired for popping a wheelie in a giant earthmoving truck, which he then plowed into Butte's main power line. He earned his nickname, "Evel," during a night in Butte's jail.

Wearing a star-spangled, red, white, and blue jumpsuit and a short shoulder cape, Knievel made millions by soaring over Mack trucks, double-decker buses, and shark-filled aquariums.

Knievel became a national celebrity in 1969 when his death-defying jump over the Caesar's Palace fountains in Las Vegas ended with a spectacular bone-breaking crash and a 29-day coma. He said: "[T]he gravest problem is that I don't lose my nerve before I jump...I'm a firm believer in the fact that any idea that a man can honestly conceive and honestly believe, if he wants to do the thing really bad enough, he can do it."

Comic books, action figures, pinball machines and movies soon immortalized his likeness. His *Guinness Book of World Records* listings included most cars jumped and most bones broken.

In 1974, Knievel made $6 million in an unsuccessful jump over the Snake River Canyon on a steam-propelled jet cycle.

Knievel retired in 1980, bragging to reporters that his body was "nothing but scar tissue and surgical steel." In 2007 he died of lung cancer. Butte celebrates his memory in their annual Evel Knievel Days.

*Evel—a nickname he loved—early in his stunt-riding career*

## KNIEVEL RECALLED:

*"I really wanted to fly through the air...I loved the thrill, the money, the whole macho thing..."*

*Excellent writer and gracious mentor James Welch*

# JAMES WELCH

**"I had had enough of Havre, enough of the town, of walking home, hung over, beaten up, or both.** I had had enough of the people, the bartenders, the bars, the cars, the hotels, but mostly, I had had enough of myself. I wanted to lose myself, to ditch these clothes, to out-run this burning sun, to stand beneath the clouds and have my shadow erased, myself along with it."

That's Montana author, James Welch, the "eminent Native American novelist," from his first book *Winter in the Blood*. The *New York Times Book Review* called it a "nearly flawless novel about human life, "praising its "young crusty dignity, its grand bare lines, its comedy and mystery, its clean pathfinding to the center of hearts."

Born in 1940 and raised on the Blackfeet and Fort Belknap reservations, Welch—a University of Montana graduate—described himself as both an "Indian writer" and "an Indian who writes." His work—wrote journalist Michael Moore—"ushered the Indian experience into the mainstream without sentimentalizing it…"

Welch's 1986 masterpiece, *Fools Crow*, told the story of a band of Blackfoot Indians in the Montana Territory of the 1870s. It won the *Los Angeles Times* Book Prize for fiction.

### WRITER IVAN DOIG DECLARED *FOOLS CROW*:

*"The single, greatest imaginative leap into a people that any of us writing here in the West have managed."*

Of his subjects Welch said: "They weren't particularly noble…[or] bad Indians. They were human beings…That's really what I wanted to get across …They weren't cliches."

Welch died in Missoula in 2003.

*A person at the base of Our Lady of the Rockies shows the statue's size.*

# OUR LADY OF THE ROCKIES

**Our Lady of the Rockies is Montana's heavy metal Madonna.**

The giant, stark white, steel and concrete statue of Mary sits atop the Continental Divide overlooking Butte. She's second only to the Statue of Liberty as America's tallest sculpture.

It started with Butte resident Bob O'Bill wanting to create a modest shrine celebrating his wife's recovery from serious illness in 1979. But O'Bill's vision soon transformed into a massive six-year community effort to erect a mountain-top landmark.

Hundreds donated materials, time, and money. O'Bill gushed: "The whole project was about volunteers…It took the whole city."

Retired miners lent their construction skills. Journalist Lynn Arave reported: "the statue's internal structure is actually an upside down mine shaft. Since…shafts were all they knew to build, that's the statue's main support."

In December of 1985, helicopters placed the final section atop the East Ridge, 3,000 feet above Montana's Mining City.

Welder Leroy Lee built the landmark without blueprints. He declared: "I didn't have a clue how to make a 90-foot statue…But there seemed to be all these little miracles along the way that got it done…[E]veryone was caught up in the spirit of accomplishing the impossible."

Today, the glowing Our Lady of the Rockies is a beacon to interstate travelers and a source of pride in Butte.

### HISTORIAN DON SPITZER BELIEVES:

*"The ninety-foot monument is more than just a religious icon. It symbolizes the fortitude and perseverance of the people in the town below."*

*Two volunteers who came to help end the Freemen standoff were, third from left, James "Bo" Gritz and, to his left, Randy Weaver, cause of the Ruby Ridge, Idaho, standoff against the FBI. Gritz had helped end Weaver's standoff, but he and Weaver left the Freemen in frustration.*

# MONTANA FREEMEN STANDOFF

**The longest armed siege in modern U.S. history took place in the Treasure State.**

The Montana Freemen were right-wing, gun-hoarding tax-protesters who declared the U.S. government illegitimate. Citing the Magna Carta and the Bible, they declared themselves "sovereign"—unanswerable to any laws, save their own.

A friend described Freemen leader Leroy Schweitzer as a "very self-sufficient, loner type…I can remember Leroy saying, 'The IRS can steal my money, but nobody else can…' That's where…his hatred of the government began."

The Freemen gathered near Jordan on a ranch they named "Justus Township." They issued "wanted dead or alive" posters and offered a million-dollar bounty for the federal judge who had foreclosed on the property. To finance it all they wrote fake "Leroy Checks" totaling $18 billion. Most were rejected, but $1.8 million worth were actually cashed—including one by the IRS.

Following Schweitzer's March 1996 arrest, his followers began an 81-day standoff. Hundreds of FBI agents surrounded the compound.

### GARFIELD COUNTY ATTORNEY NICK MURNION STATED:

*"I believe this group has declared war on our form of government… They are in open insurrection."*

Rather than triggering a gun battle, FBI agents waited. Finally, negotiators convinced the Freemen to surrender peacefully. Officials charged the ringleaders with forty federal offences. Juries convicted several—including Schweitzer.

*The determined Elouise Pepion Cobell bore the Indian name Yellow Bird Woman*

# ELOUISE COBELL

**Commenting on Blackfoot elder-activist Elouise Cobell's ground-breaking legal challenge on behalf of native peoples everywhere**, the *Great Falls Tribune* predicted: "[She] will go down in history as the woman who won recognition and respect for her people who had been cheated…by the federal government since the late 1800s."

She was the great-granddaughter of famed warrior Mountain Chief, and grew up on Montana's Blackfeet Reservation. As the tribe's treasurer, Cobell—also known as Yellow Bird Woman—uncovered "a shocking pattern of deception." The U.S. government had underpaid Indian nations in the billions of dollars for royalties on oil, gas, timber and grazing leases.

## COBELL SAID:

*"It's just such a wrong that if I didn't do something about it I'm as criminal as the government."*

In 1996, Cobell filed one of the largest class action lawsuits ever. After fifteen years of litigation, she and her attorneys won a $3.4 billion settlement, benefitting nearly 300,000 Native Americans.

Judge Royce Lamberth called the case: "a story shot through with bureaucratic blunders…and peppered with scandals[,]…dirty tricks and outright villainy…" Cobell said: "I never started this case with any intentions of being a hero. I just wanted…to give justice to people that didn't have it."

Cobell had given up her post as president of Montana's Elvis Presley fan club to pursue the lawsuit. When she died in October 2011, she was buried with a rosary, a braid of sweetgrass, and an Elvis doll.

*In 1908, the Bobcat and Grizzly varsity football teams met for this game at the University of Montana, in Missoula.* MANSFIELD LIBRARY, UNIVERSITY OF MONTANA

# THE CAT-GRIZ RIVALRY

**The Cat-Griz rivalry between Montana State and Montana is one of this country's oldest interstate football matchups.** Fans call it the "Brawl of the Wild."

Sportswriter Colter Nuanez once observed: "[It] isn't just a football game. It's a cultural event. It's a defining day for residents all across the Treasure State."

Bozeman and Missoula first fought on the gridiron in 1897. Journalist Bill Speltz wrote: "Over the years [they've tried] almost anything to get each other's goat. Flea-flickers, halfback passes, double reverses—you're bound to see something unusual each time they meet…"

### SPORTSWRITER DUSTIN ASKIM WROTE:

*"No other small state has a rivalry like this…Score changes can be heard echoing from the mountains…to the prairies…"*

Montana wide receiver Sam Gratton said: "It's like Red Sox–Yankees times 10…" Former Bobcat, now New England Patriot, Dane Fletcher declared: "You're not half Bobcat, you're not half Griz. You're one or the other…If you say you're half-and-half, then you're not a true Montanan."

In Bobcat coach Rob Ash's words: "Cat-Griz is every day of the year… not just in the football sense, but as a way of life…You are always competing…You go anywhere…and a guy sees your Bobcat plates on your car and he's a Bobcat, he loves you. If he's a Griz, he hates you. It's just the way it is. It's all year, 365 days."

University of Montana led the series 70-37-5 as of 2013.

# BIBLIOGRAPHY

## Newspapers

A Freight Train Slaughters 36—Shocking Collision of the Great Northern at Nyack, Mont.," *Chateauguay Record* (New York) 9-6-1901.

"A Millionaire Miner's Wedding," *The New York Times,* March 3, 1886.

"A Terrific Explosion—Several Cars Of Powder Ignited Burning A Butte Fire—Fire Department Wiped Out," *The Evening News.* (Lincoln, NE) 16 January 1895.

Baumler, Ellen. "The Mysterious Death of Senator Thomas Walsh," *Independent Record* (Helena), December 24, 2000, 1C.

Briggeman, Kim. "Missoula Witness to History of Industrial Workers of the World," *Missoulian.* September 2, 2009.

—. "Montana History Almanac: Gold Rush in Full Swing at Bannack," *Missoulian* July 23, 2011.

—. "Montana History Almanac: Stuart Shoots Antelope While Fending for Self," Missoulian June 04, 2011.

—. "Montana history almanac: Fort Keogh noted for cold, snowflakes," *Missoulian*, January 9, 2011.

—. "Montana History Almanac: Virginia City Boxing Match Ends in Draw" *Missoulian*, January 2, 2011.

—. "Montana History Almanac: Western Icon Fort Union Closes Shop," *Missoulian*, August 9, 2009.

—. "Montana History Almanac: Senator Decries U.S. Reds, Radicals," *Missoulian*, May 31, 2009.

—. "Montana History Almanac: Big Burn of 1910 Blows Up, Fueled by Furious Winds," *Missoulian,* August 17, 2008.

—. "Montana History Almanac: Toasts, Songs Mark Arrival of First Trains," *Missoulian*, April 08, 2008.

—. "Montana History Almanac: Fort Union was 'King' of Missouri Fur Trade in 1800s," *Missoulian*, October 14, 2007.

—. "Montana History Almanac: Lewis First Laid Eyes on Great Falls in June 1805," *Missoulian*, June 10, 2007.

—. "Montana History Almanac: 1908 Flood Swallowed Higgins Avenue Bridge," *Missoulian*, June 03, 2007.

—. "Montana History Almanac: Montana Shaped by Enlarged Homestead Act," *Missoulian*, February 18, 2007.

—. "Montana History Almanac: Devastating blaze roared through Helena in 1874," *Missoulian*, January 07, 2007.

Brooke, James. "Anti-Government Freemen Are Found Guilty of Fraud," *The New York Times,* July 3, 1998, A12.

—. "Prosecutors Tell Jurors that Freemen Case Is About Fraud, Not Politics," *The New York Times,* May 29, 1998, A12.

Clark, Helen. "Montana's Most Notorious Outlaws," *The Montana Journal,* May-June 1992, 13.

Coates, Grace Stone. "The Story of Charles M. Bair, Great Flockmaster of Montana," n.d. Montana Historical Society Vertical Files, Montana Historical Society, Helena, Montana.

"The Crow Outbreak—Sitting Bull's Fiery Speech is Now Bearing Fruit," *The New York Times,* October 7, 1887.

Culbertson, Joseph. "Joseph Culbertson Tells of Life of His Father, Who Built Fort Benton," n. d. Montana Historical Society Vertical Files, Montana Historical Society, Helena, Montana.

Culum, Marjorie A. "Native Son Always Proud of Birthplace," *The Independent Record (Helena),* June 25, 1961.

Cummings, Rial. "Nothing Golden Can Stay," *The Missoulian*, February 13, 2005.

"Damage by Western Flood," *Wall Street Journal* April 16, 1908.

"Dead Sure Enough—Paulsen Story from Butte Thoroughly Punctured," *The Minneapolis Journal* March 29, 1902.

"Death Toll in Train Wreck Will Be Between 40 and 60; Cranes Raising the Coaches," *Marysville (Ohio) Tribune,* June 20, 1938.

"Declares Sedition Steadily Spreading—Senator Myers Asserts Sympathizers with Radicals Are Found 'in High Places,'" *The New York Times*, April 29, 1920.

"The Dissatisfied Crows—Trouble with a Peaceful Tribe of Indians," *The New York Times*, October 16, 1887, 10.

"Feigns Death to Escape Law—Former Montana Architect Declared to be Living," *The San Francisco Call* March 29, 1902.

"Fire in Helena, Montana" *The New York Times* January 10, 1874.

"'Floppin' Bill' Cantrell was a Terror to Indians, Cattle Rustlers, and Horse Thieves in Central and Northern Montana," *The Park County News* n .d. Montana Historical Society Vertical Files, Montana Historical Society, Helena, Montana.

Giles, Kevin. "The Belle of Women's Rights and the Champion of Causes Remembers," *The Independent Record (Helena)*, October 10, 1976, 33.

Glynn, Gary. "Landusky Meets Kid Curry," *The Montana Journal*, March-April 1992, 5.

Goldberg, Carey. "Last of Freemen Surrender to F. B. I. at Montana Site," *New York Times*, June 14, 1996.

Goldstein, Richard. "Dave McNally, 60, Early Free Agent, Dies," *The New York Times*, December 3, 2002.

Grill, Mon Tana Lou, "Pierre Wibaux," *Redstone Review, June 13, 1930.*

Hillinger, Charles. "Camaraderie Keynotes Devil's Brigade Reunion," *The Los Angeles Times*. August 31, 1986.

"Historical Fact Inaccuracy Re Yankee Jim, Indian Taboo in Park Irks Lon Garrison," *Park County News (Livingston)* May 31, 1962.

"Hunting Horse Thieves—Montana Overrun with Bands of Lawless Men," *The New York Times*, December 14, 1884.

Hurd, N. C. "Pierre Wibaux, Largest Cattle Rancher in World," Montana Historical Society Vertical Files, Montana Historical Society, Helena, Montana.

"I. W. W. Strike Chief Lynched At Butte." *The New York Times*. August 2, 1917.

"Joseph Medicine Crow, 95, Oldest Member of Montana Tribe," *Great Falls Tribune*, August 13, 2009, 1m.

"Kirby Grant, 'Sky King,' Killed in Auto Accident," *The Orlando Sentinel*, October 31, 1985.

Klepper, Don F. "Midnight Calamity at Saugus," *The Montana Journal*, March-April 1992, p. 7.

"Leader Restoring Bison to Indians—Robert Yellowtail in Valley of Little Big Horn is Building a 'New Empire' for the Crows," *New York Times*, August 23, 1936, N6.

Lefohn, Phyllis and Arnie Malina. "A Tribute to a Writer," *The Independent Record (Helena)*, May 8, 1985.

Miller, Robert E. "Helena to Rebuild with Eye to Quake," *The New York Times* October 27, 1935.

"Montana's Murray Dies in Butte," *The Great Falls Tribune*, March 24, 1961.

"More Than Forty Killed—Explosions at Butte Terribly Destructive of Life," *The New York Times* (New York, NY) 17 January 1895.

"Movies Arraigned by Senator Myers," *The New York Times*, June 30, 1922.

"Mrs. Evelyn Cameron, Pioneer of Eastern Montana," Passed Away in Hospital at Glendive," *News* Montana Historical Society Vertical Files, Montana Historical Society, Helena, Montana.

"Myers Bolts State Ticket in Montana," *The New York Times*, September 28, 1920.

"Pierre Wibaux Passed Away in Chicago Hospital Last Friday," Montana Historical Society Vertical Files, Montana Historical Society, Helena, Montana.

Pomplun, Ray. "Chief Gall," *The Denver Post*, January 9, 1977, 29 and 31.

Pound, Arthur. "The Grandfather of Montana," *The New York Times*, June 13, 1926.

Randall, Gay. "Yankee Jim of Yellowstone Toll Road Fame Made a President come to Him," *Spokesman-Review*, July 25, 1954, 8-9.

Rimel, Ira W. "Natawista Culbertson," *Montana Journal, 5:4* July-August 1991, 1-2.

Schontzler, Gail. "Colorful Madams: Bozeman's Red Right District Thrived for 50 Years," *Bozeman Daily Chronicle*, May 9, 2011.

"Scout Curley Dies; Custer Survivor," *Billings Gazette*, May 24, 1923.

"Senator Myers Deplores Police Unions; Predicts Move Here for Soviet Rule," *The New York Times*, September 12, 1919.

"Senators Petition Truman on Jews," *The New York Times*, May 4, 1947.

"Sitting Bull's Rival—Chief Gall's Speech at a Council of the Sioux." *The New York Times*, November 3, 1887.

"Sword Bearer is Slain," *The New York Times*, November 7, 1887.

"Tommy Cruise's Happy Year—The Rich Montana Miner Mourning the Early Loss of his Wife," *The New York Times*, May 8, 1887.

"The Troublesome Crows," *The New York Times*, November 19, 1887, 5.

"Train Wreck Toll Mounts To 56 Dead, 67 Hurt—Smashed Coaches Are Pulled From Waters Of Creek," *The Ogden Standard Examiner* (Utah) 6-20-1938

Trainor, Tim. "Butte's Iconic Our lady of the Rockies Celebrates Twenty-Five Years," *Montana Standard*, December 18, 2010.

"Tremors Ravage 500-mile Area; 2 Die in Helena," *The Washington Post* November 1, 1935.

Tribune Staff. "125 Montana Newsmakers," *Great Falls Tribune*. 125th Anniversary Feature. Greatfallstribune.com. Retrieved August 28, 2011.

"Two Towns Swept By Montana Flood," *The New York Times*, April 16, 1908.

West, Ed. "Baseball Great Dave McNally Dies in Billings," *Billings Gazette*, December 1, 2002.

"Western Rivers Up," *The New York Times* June 6, 1908.

Wright, Jerry. "Helena Loses a Great Lady—Activist Belle Winestine Dies," *The Independent Record (Helena)* April 22, 1985.

"Yankee Jim Built Toll Road Leading Into Yellowstone Park…," *Rocky Mountain American*, August 20, 1934.

## Websites

http://www.gendisasters.com/mt/

http://chroniclingamerica.loc.gov/

## Dissertations, Theses, and Unpublished Papers

Frisch, Paul. "The 'Gibraltar of Unionism': The Working Class at Butte, Montana, 1878-1906," Ph.D. diss., University of California, Los Angeles, 1992.

Garrity, Donald A. "The Frank Little Episode and the Butte Labor Troubles of 1917." B. A. thesis, Carroll College, April 1957.

Gutfeld, Arnon. "The Butte Labor Strikes and Company Retaliation During World War I," M. A. Thesis, University of Montana, 1967.

Smith, Norma. "The Rise and Fall of the Butte Miner's Union, 1878-1914," M. A. Thesis, Montana State University, Bozeman, 1961.

## Books

Abbott, Edward Charles. *We Pointed Them North: Recollection of a Cowpuncher.* Ed. by Helena Huntington Smith. Normanlahoma: University of Oklahoma Press, 1939.

Alderson, Nannie T. and Helena Huntington Smith. *A Bride Goes West.* Lincoln: University of Nebraska Press, 1942.

Ambrose, Stephen. *Undaunted Courage: Meriwether Lewis, Thomas Jefferson, and the Opening of the American West.* New York: Touchstone Press, 1996.

Astle, John. *Only in Butte: Stories Off the Hill.* Butte, MT: Holt Publishing Group, 2004.

Axline, Jon, et. al. *More from the Quarries of Last Chance Gulch.* Helena: Independent Record, 1995.

—. *More from the Quarries of Last Chance Gulch, Volume II.* Helena, MT: Independent Record, 1996.

Barbour, Barton H. *Fort Union and the Upper Missouri Fur Trade.* Norman: University of Oklahoma Press, 2002.

Baumler, Ellen. *Montana Moments: History on the Go.* Helena: Montana Historical Society Press, 2010.

- -. *More Montana Moments.* Helena: Montana Historical Society Press, 2012.

Bevis, William. "Nannie Alderson's Frontiers—and Ours," *Montana: The Magazine of Western History* 39:2 (Spring 1989), 29-33.

Brown, Mark H. *The Plainsmen of the Yellowstone: A History of the Yellowstone Basin.* Lincoln: University of Nebraska Press, 1961.

Bryan, William L. *Montana's Indians: Yesterday and Today.* Helena, MT: American and World Geographic Publishing, 1996.

Burlingame, Merrill. *The Montana Frontier.* Bozeman, MT: Big Sky Books, 1980.

Burlingame, Merrill G., and K. Ross Toole. *History of Montana.* 3 vols. New York: Lewis Historical Publishing Co., 1957.

Calkins, Ray. *Looking Back from the Hill.* Butte, Montana: Butte Historical Society, 1982.

Calloway, Colin G. (ed.) *Our Hearts Fell to the Ground: Plains Indian Views of How the West was Lost.* Boston: Bedford/St. Martins Press, 1996.

Calvert, Jerry. *The Gibraltar: Socialism and Labor in Butte, Montana, 1895-1920.* Helena: Montana Historical Society Press, 1988.

Cheney, Roberta Carkeek. *Names on the Face of Montana: The Story of Montana's Place Names.* Rev. ed. Missoula: Mountain Press Publishing Co., 1984.

*Contributions to the Historical Society of Montana (10 volumes)* (Helena: Montana Historical Society). 1876-1940.

Crutchfield, James A. *It Happened in Montana.* Guilford, CT: The Globe Pequot Press, 2008.

Denig, Edwin Thompson. *Five Indian Tribes of the Upper Missouri: Sioux, Arickaras, Assiniboines, Crees, Crows*, ed. by John C. Ewers. Norman: University of Oklahoma Press, 1961.

*Dictionary of American Biography.* New York: Charles Scribner's Sons, 1930, vols. 1- 5.

Dimsdale, Thomas J. *The Vigilantes of Montana.* Norman: University of Oklahoma Press, 1953.

Emmons, David M. *The Butte Irish: Class and Ethnicity in an American Mining Town, 1875-1925.* Urbana: University of Illinois Press, 1989.

Gates, Henry Louis (ed.) *African American National Biography.* London: Oxford University Press, 208.

Gutfeld, Arnon. *Montana's Agony: Years of War and Hysteria, 1917-21.* Gainesville: University Presses of Florida, 1979.

Haines, Aubrey L. *Yellowstone Story: A History of Our First National Park*. 2 vols. Yellowstone National Park, Wyo.: Yellowstone Library and Museum Association in Cooperation with Colorado Associated University Press, 1977.

Harvie. Robert A. *Keeping the Peace: Police Reform in Montana*, 1889 to 1918. Helena: Montana Historical Society Press, 1994.

Hine, Darline Clark Hine (ed.) *Black Women in America*, 2nd Edition. London: Oxford University Press, 2005.

Holmes, Krys. *Montana: Stories of the Land*. Helena: Montana Historical Society Press, 2009.

Howard, Joseph Kinsey. *Montana: High, Wide, and Handsome*. New Haven: Yale University Press, 1943.

—. *Montana Margins: A State Anthology*. New Haven, CT: Yale University Press, 1946.

Hoxie, Frederick E. *Parading Through History: The Making of the Crow Nation*, 1805-1935. Cambridge, England: Cambridge University Press, 1995.

Johnson, Dorothy. *The Bloody Bozeman: The Perilous Trail to Montana's Gold*. Mountain Press Publishing Co., 1983.

Keenan, Jerry. *The Life of Yellowstone Kelly*. Albuquerque, NM: University of New Mexico Press, 2006.

Kidston, Martin J. *Cromwell Dixon: A Boy and his Plane*, 1892-1911. Helena, MT: Farcountry Press, 2007.

Kittridge, William and Annick Smith, eds. *The Last Best Place: A Montana Anthology*. Seattle: University Washington Press, 1988; Helena: Montana Historical Society Press, 1988.

Kohl, Martha. *I Do: A Cultural History of Montana Weddings*. Helena: Montana Historical Society Press, 2011.

Lamar, Howard R. *The New Encyclopedia of the American West*. New Haven, CT: Yale University Press, 1998.

Langford, Nathaniel Pitt. *Vigilante Days and Way—The Pioneers of the Rockies*. New York: D. D. Merrill, 1893.

Laskin, David. *The Children's Blizzard*. New York: Harper-Collins Publishers, 2004.

Linderman, Frank B. *Pretty Shield: Medicine Woman of the Crows*. Lincoln: University of Nebraska Press, 1932.

Logan, Rayford W. and Michael R. Winston. *Dictionary of American Negro Biography*. New York: W. W. Norton and Company, 1983.

McLoughlin, Denis. *Wild and Woolly: An Encyclopedia of the Old West*, Garden City, NY: Doubleday and Company, Inc, 1975.

Malone, Michael P. *The Battle for Butte: Mining and Politics on the Northern Frontier, 1864-1906*. Seattle: University of Washington Press, 1981.

—, Richard B. Roeder, and William L. Lang. *Montana: A History of Two Centuries*. Revised Edition. Seattle: University Washington Press, 1991.

Mercier, Laurie. *Anaconda: Labor, Community, and Culture in Montana's Smelter City*. Urbana: University of Illinois Press, 2001.

Milner, Clyde A. and Carol A. O'Conner. *As Big as the West: The Pioneer Life of Granville Stuart*. New York: Oxford University Press, 2008.

Missoulian. *100 Montanans: Our Pick For the Most Influential Figures of the 20th Century*. Missoula, MT: Missoulian, 2000.

Montana Historical Society, ed. *Not in Precious Metals Alone: A Manuscript History of Montana*. Helena: Montana Historical Society Press, 1976.

Morris, Patrick F. *Anaconda: Copper Smelting Boom Town on the Western Frontier*, Bethesda: Swan Publishing, 1997.

Morrison, John, and Catherine Wright Morrison. *Mavericks: The Lives and Battles of Montana's Political Mavericks*. Helena: Montana Historical Press, 2003.

Murphy, Mary. *Mining Cultures: Men Women and Leisure in Butte, 1914-41*. Urbana: University of Illinois Press, 1997.

Neihardt, John G. *Black Elk Speaks: Being the Life Story of a Holy Man of the Ogalala Sioux as Told Through John G. Neihardt (Premier Edition)* Albany: State University of New York Press, 2008.

Parry, Ellis Robert. *Montana Dateline*. Guilford, CT: Globe Pequot Press, 2001.

Petrik, Paula. *No Step Backward: Women and Family on the Rocky Mountain Mining Frontier, Helena, Montana, 1865-1900*. Helena: Montana Historical Society, 1987.

Phillips, Charles and Alan Axelrod. *Encyclopedia of the American West, Volumes 1-3.* New York: Simon and Schuster Macmillan, 1996.

*Progressive Men of the State of Montana.* Chicago: A. W. Bowden & Co., 1902.

Punke, Michael. *Fire and Brimstone: The North Butte Mining Disaster of 1917.* New York: Hyperion Books, 2006.

—. *Last Stand: George Bird Grinnell, the Battle to Save the Buffalo, and the Birth of the New West.* Lincoln, Nebraska: University of Nebraska Press, 2009.

Raymer, Robert G. *Montana: The Land and the People.* Chicago and New York: Lewis Publishing Company, 1930.

Sanders, Helen F. *History of Montana.* Chicago, IL: Lewis Publishing Company, 1913.

Searl, Molly. *Montana Disasters: Fires, Floods, and Other Catastrophes.* Boulder, CO: Pruett Publishing. 2001.

Smith, Jeffrey. *Montana Book of Days: 365 Days—365 Stories: The Short Course in Montana History.* Missoula, MT: Historic Montana Publishing, 2003.

Smith, Victor Grant. *The Champion Buffalo Hunter: The Frontier Memoirs of Yellowstone Vic Smith.* Helena, MT: Twodot Press, 1997.

Spritzer, Don. *Roadside History of Montana.* Missoula: Mountain Press Publishing Company, 1999.

Swartout, Robert R. Jr. and Harry W. Fritz. *The Montana Heritage: An Anthology of Historical Essays.* Helena: Montana Historical Society Press, 1992.

Taylor, Quintard. *In Search of the Racial Frontier: African Americans in the American West, 1528-1990.* New York: W. W. Norton, 1998.

Thompson, Larry S. *Montana's Explorers: The Pioneer Naturalists.* Helena: Montana Magazine, 1985.

Thrapp, Dan L. *Enclyopedia of Frontier Biography* (3 vols.). Lincoln, Nebraska: University of Nebraska Press, 1988.

Toole, K. Ross *Montana: An Uncommon Land.* Norman, University of Oklahoma Press, 1959.

—. *20th Century Montana: A State of Extremes.* Norman: University of Oklahoma Press, 1983.

Van West, Carroll. *A Traveler's Companion to Montana History*. Helena: Montana Historical Society Press, 1986.

Walter, Dave. *Montana Campfire Tales: Fourteen Historical Narratives*. Helena, MT: Falcon Publishing, 1997.

—. *More Montana Campfire Tales: Fifteen Historical Narratives*. Helena, MT: Farcountry Press, 2002.

Walter, Dave., ed. *Speaking Ill of the Dead: Jerks in Montana History*. Helena, MT: Falcon Publishing, 2000.

—. *Still Speaking Ill of the Dead: More Jerks in Montana History*. Helena, MT: Globe Pequot Press, 2005.

Welch, James and Stekler, Paul. *Killing Custer: The Battle of the Little Big Horn and the Fate of the Plains Indians*. New York: W. W. Norton, 1994.

Wilson, Gary A. *Outlaw Tales of Montana: True Stories of Notorious Montana Bandits, Culprits, and Crooks*. Guiford, Conn: The Globe Pequot Press, 2003.

Wishart, David J. *Encyclopedia of the Great Plains*. Lincoln: University of Nebraska Press, 2004.

Wischmann, Lesley. *Frontier Diplomats: The Life and Times of Alexander Culbertson and Natoyist-Siksina*. Spokane, WA: The Arthur H. Clark Company, 2000.

Wright, John B. *Montana Places: Exploring Big Sky Country*. Minneapolis, MN: University of Minnesota Press, 2000.

## Articles

Allen, Frederick. "Montana Vigilantes and the Origins of 3-7-77," *Montana: The Magazine of Western History*, 51:1 (Spring 2001), 2-19.

Alonso, Harriet Hyman. "Jeannette Rankin and the Women's Peace Union." *Montana: The Magazine of Western History* 39:2 (Spring 1989): 34-49.

Anderson, Irving W. "Profiles of the American West—A Charbonneau Family Portrait," *American West* 17 (March/April 1980), 4-13, 63.

Athearn, Robert G., "The Civil War and Montana Gold: The Great War Muddies the Mountain Waters," *Montana: The Magazine of Western History*, 12:2, Civil War in the West (Spring 1962), 62-73.

Bakken, Gordon Morris and Bakken, J. Elwood. "The Goldfish Died: Great Falls, Fort Benton, and the Great Flood of 1908," *Montana: The Magazine of*

*Western History* 51:4 (Winter 2001), 38-51.

Bates, J. Leonard. "Thomas J. Walsh: His 'Genius for Controversy,'" *Montana: The Magazine of Western History* 19:4 (Autumn 1969), 2-15.

Behan, Barbara Carol. "Forgotten Heritage: African Americans in the Montana Territory, 1864-1889," *The Journal of African American History*, 91:1, The African American Experience in the Western States (Winter 2006), 23-40.

Boeve, Eunice. "Pasttimes—Mary Fields: The Tough, Tender Legend of Cascade," *Montana Magazine* 165 (January/February 2001), 70-74.

Bowers, E. H. "Water Rodeo," *Milwaukee Magazine* (September 1941), 5.

Brown, Mark H. and Felton, W. R. "L. A. Huffman: Brady of the West," *Montana: The Magazine of Western History*, 6:1 (Winter 1956), 29-37.

Burlingame, Merrill G. "The Influence of the Military in the Building of Montana," *The Pacific Northwest Quarterly*, 29:2 (Apr., 1938), 135-150.

—. "Montana's Righteous Hangmen: A Reconsideration," *Montana: The Magazine of Western History*, 28:4 (Autumn 1978), 36-49.

Burt, Larry. "Nowhere Left to Go: Montana's Crees, Metis, and Chippewas and the Creation of Rocky Boy's Reservation," *Great Plains Quarterly 7* (Summer 1987), 195-209.

Calloway, Collin G. "Sword Bearer and the 'Crow Outbreak,' 1887," *Montana: The Magazine of Western History* 36:4 (August 1986), 38-51.

Calvert, Jerry. "The Rise and Fall of Socialism in a Company Town, 1902-1920," *Montana: The Magazine of Western History* 36 (Autumn 1986): 2.

Chadwick, Robert A. "Montana's Silver Mining Era: Great Boom and Great Bust." *Montana: The Magazine of Western History* 32 (Spring 1982): 16-31.

Coleman, Rufus. "Mark Twain in Montana, 1895," *Montana: The Magazine of History*, 3:2 (Spring 1953), 9-17.

Doyle, Susan Badger. "Indian Perspectives of the Bozeman Trail," *Montana: The Magazine of Western History*, 40:1 (Winter 1990), 56-67.

—. "Journeys to the Land of Gold: Emigrants on the Bozeman Trail, 1863-1866," *Montana: The Magazine of Western History*, 41:4 (Autumn 1991): 54-67.

Dusenberry, Verne. "An Appreciation of James Willard Schultz," *Montana: The Magazine of Western History* 10:4 (Autumn 1960), 22-23.

—. "The Rocky Boy Indians: Montana's Displaced People" *Montana: The Magazine of Western History* 4(1) 1954, 1-15.

Dubofsky, Melvin. "The Origins of Western Working Class Radicalism, 1890-1905," *Labor History* (1966): 140.

Evans, William B. "James E. Murray: A Voice of the People in Foreign Affaires," *Montana: The Magazine of Western History* 32:1 (Winter 1982), 24-35.

Everett, George "The Gibraltar of Unionism: The Labor Heritage of Butte, Montana," *Labor's Heritage* (Summer 1998): 6-19.

Flaherty, Stacy A. "Boycott in Butte: Organized Labor and the Chinese Community, 1896-1897," *Montana: The Magazine of Western History*, 37:1 (Winter 1987), 34-47.

Fogde, Myron J. "Brother Van's Call to Frontier Montana," *Montana: The Magazine of Western History*, 22:4 (Autumn 1972), 2-15.

Frisch, Paul. "Gibraltar of Unionism: The Development of Butte's Labor Movement," *The Speculator* 2 (Summer 1985): 12-20.

Furtwangler, Albert. "Sacajawea's Son as a Symbol," *Oregon Historical Quarterly* 102:3 (Fall 2001), 290-315.

Goodstein, Phil H. "The Rise of the Rocky Mountain Labor Movement: Militant Industrial Unionism and the Western Federation of Miners," *Labor's Heritage*, (July 1990): 21-33.

Gutfeld, Arnon. "The Murder of Frank Little: Radical Labor Agitation in Butte, Montana, 1917." *Labor History* 10 (Spring 1969): 177-92.

—. "The Speculator Disaster in 1917: Labor Resurgence at Butte, Montana." *Arizona and the West* 11 (Spring 1969): 27-38.

Hampton, Bruce. "Battle of the Big Hole," *Montana: The Magazine of Western History*, 44:1 (Winter 1994), 2-13.

—. "Battle of the Big Hole: Part Two," *Montana: The Magazine of Western History*, 44:2 (Spring 1994), 18-29.

Holien, Mick. "110 Battles and Counting," *Montana Magazine* 224 (November-December 2010), 72-75.

Jannotta, Sepp. "The Man Who Saved Millions," *Mountains and Minds: The Montana State University Magazine*. (Fall 2012).

Johnson, Dorothy. "Durable Desperado Kid Curry," *Montana: The Magazine of Western History*, 6:2 (Spring 1956), 22-31.

——. (ed.) and Fred Whiteside. "The Graft that Failed," *Montana: The Magazine of Western History* 9:4 (Autumn 1959), 2-11.

Johnson, Marc C. "Mike Mansfield: Defining Character," *Montana Magazine* 172 (March-April 2002), 18-21.

Keenan, Jerry. "Yellowstone Kelly: From New York to Paradise," *Montana: The Magazine of Western History*, 40:3 (Summer 1990), 14-27.

Lang, William L. "Spoils of Statehood: Montana Communities in Conflict, 1888-1894," *Montana: The Magazine of Western History*, 37:4, The Centennial West: Politics (Autumn 1987), 34-45.

Larson, Robert W. "Part 1: Red Cloud: The Warrior Years," *Montana: The Magazine of Western History*, 47:1 (Spring 1997), 22-31.

——. "Part II: Red Cloud: The Reservation Years," *Montana: The Magazine of Western History*, 47:2 (Summer 1997), 14-25.

Lindau, Paul, and Frederic Trautmann. "Across Montana on the Northern Pacific in 1883," *Montana: The Magazine of Western History*, 35:2 (Spring 1985), 60-65.

Lips, Jerry. "From Out of the Clear Blue of the Western Sky Comes . . . Sky King," *Airport Journals*, January 1, 2006.

Lucey, Donna M. "The Intimate Vision of Evelyn Cameron," *Geo* (January 1983), 67-78.

Lukacs, John D. "Everybody's All Americans," *Mountains and Minds—The Montana State University Magazine*. (Fall 2012).

Mattern, Carolyn J. "Mary MacLane: A Feminist Opinion," *Montana: The Magazine of Western History* 24:4 (Autumn 1977), 54-63.

Miller, Barbara. " 'Hot as Live Embers—Cold as Hail': The Restless Soul of Butte's Mary MacLane," *Montana Magazine*, September 1982, 50-53.

Milner, Darrell. "York of the Corps of Discovery: Interpretations of York's Character and His Role in the Lewis and Clark Expedition," Oregon Historical Quarterly, 104:3 (Fall, 2003), 302-333.

Mullen, Pierce C. and Nelson, Michael L. "Montanans and "The Most Peculiar Disease: The Influenza Epidemic and Public Health, 1918-1919," *Montana: The Magazine of Western History,* 37:2 (Spring 1987), 50-61.

Murphy, Mary, "Bootlegging Mothers and Drinking Daughters: Gender and Prohibition in Butte, Montana," *American Quarterly,* 46:2, (June, 1994), 174-94.

Nash, Roderick, "The Strenuous Life of Bob Marshall," *Forest History,* 10:3 (Oct., 1966), 18-25.

O'Neil, Carle F. "Pacific Memories: Montana National Guardsmen Recall the Fighting on New Guinea in World War II," *Montana: The Magazine of Western History,* 52:2, Special Fly-Fishing Issue (Summer 2002), 48-57.

Parrett, Aaron. Montana's Worst Natural Disaster: The 1964 Flood on the Blackfeet Indian Reservation *Montana: The Magazine of Western History,* 54:2 (Summer 2004), 20-31.

Peterson, Jim. "The West is Burning Up—The 1910 Fire," *Evergreen Magazine.* Winter Edition 1994-1995.

Petrik, Paula. "Capitalists with Rooms: Prostitution in Helena, Montana, 1865-1900," *Montana: The Magazine of Western History,* 31:2 (Spring 1981), 28-41.

Poten, Constance J. "Robert Yellowtail, the New Warrior," *Montana: The Magazine of Western History,* 39:3 (Summer 1989), 36-41.

Renner, Ginger K. "Charlie and the Ladies in His Life," *Montana: The Magazine of Western History,* 34:3, Charles M. Russell: A Special Issue (Summer 1984), 34-61.

Ritchie, Donald A. "The Senate of Mike Mansfield." *Montana: The Magazine of Western History* 48 (Winter 1998): 50-62.

Roeder, Richard B. "Crossing the Gender Line: Ella L. Knowles, Montana's First Woman Lawyer," *Montana: The Magazine of Western History,* 32:3 (Summer 1982), 64-75.

—. "A Settlement on the Plains: Paris Gibson and the Building of Great Falls," *Montana: The Magazine of Western History,* 42:4 (Autumn 1992), 4-19.

Rostad, Lee and David Lamb. "Charley Bair: King of Western Sheepmen," *Montana: The Magazine of Western History,* 20:4 (Autumn 1970), 50-61.

Schemmn, Mildred Walker. "The Major's Lady: Natawista." *Montana: The Magazine of Western History*, 2:1, January 1952, 5-15.

Shovers, Brian. "The Perils of Working in the Butte Underground: Industrial Fatalities in the Copper Mines, 1880-1920." *Montana: The Magazine of Western History* 37 (Spring 1987): 26-39.

Smith, Phyllis. "'Peas That Please': The Gallatin Valley Pea Industry, 1911-1970," *Montana: The Magazine of Western History*, 58:2 (Summer 2008), 60-69, 99.

Snow, Don. "Writing the Real Montana—James Willard Schultz: In the Crease of Time," 159 *Montana Magazine* (January/February 2000), 13-21.

Staudohar, Connie. "'Food, Rest, & Happyness'": Limitations and Possibilities in the Early Treatment of Tuberculosis in Montana, Part I," *Montana: The Magazine of Western History*, 47:4 (Winter 1997), 48-57.

—. "'Food, Rest, & Happyness'": Limitations and Possibilities in the Early Treatment of Tuberculosis in Montana, Part II," *Montana: The Magazine of Western History*, 48:1 (Spring 1998), 44-55.

—. "The 320 Ranch," *Montana: The Magazine of Western History*, 55:2 (Summer 2005), 75-77.

Thane, James L. Jr. "The Montana "Indian War" of 1867," *Arizona and the West*, 10:2 (Summer 1968), 153-170.

Venn, George A. "The Wobblies and Montana's Garden City," *Montana: The Magazine of Western History*, 21:4 (Autumn 1971), 18-30.

Walter, Dave. "Butte Paradise: Columbia Gardens." *Montana Magazine* 73 (September-October 1985), 22-27.

—. "Final Hour: Sunset for the American Bison," *Montana Magazine* 92 (November-December 1988), 52-58.

—. "Floppin Bill Cantrell," *Montana Magazine* 99 (January-February 1990), 50-53.

—. "PastTimes—Courtland DuRand Wrangles the Dude…." *Montana Magazine* 156 (July-August 1999), 88-95.

—. "PastTimes—Fred Whiteside: Beyond the Reach of Millions," *Montana Magazine* 188 (November/December 1988), 62-66.

—. "PastTimes—Weaving the Current: Montana's Watershed Events of Two Centuries, Parts 1-6," *Montana Magazine*, 158-164 (January-February through November-December 2000): various pages.

Wheeler, Leslie A., "Montana's Shocking 'Lit'ry Lady'," *Montana: The Magazine of Western History* 27 (Summer 1977), 20-33.

White, W. Thomas. "Paris Gibson, James J. Hill & the "New Minneapolis": The Great Falls Water Power and Townsite Company, 1882-1908," *Montana: The Magazine of Western History*, 33:3 (Summer 1983), 60-69.

Wiltsey, Norman "Plenty Coups: Statesman Chief of the Crows," *Montana: The Magazine of Western History*, 13:4 (Autumn 1963):. 28-39.

Winestine, Belle Fligelman. "Mother Was Shocked," *Montana: The Magazine of Western History*, 24:3 (Summer 1974), 70-79.

\* \* \* \*

# ABOUT THE AUTHOR

B. Derek Strahn is a historian, high school teacher, historic preservation consultant, freelance writer, and folk/blues musician. Since 2008 he has researched, written, and narrated the *Montana Medicine Show*, a weekly radio broadcast from KGLT Studios on the campus of Montana State University in Bozeman. He lives in Bozeman with his wife and three sons.

# INDEX